The Good Fight:

Our Battle with Cancer

Kimberly Hritz

NEW INTERNATIONAL VERSION. Copyright © 1973, 1978, 1984 by International Bible Society

Copyright © 2009 Kimberly Hritz

All rights reserved. No part of this publication may be reproduced, stored in a retrieval system, or transmitted in any form or by any means, electronic, mechanical, photocopying, recording, or otherwise, without the prior written permission of the publisher.

ISBN:978-1-60383-224-3

Published by:
Holy Fire Publishing
Unit 116
1525-D Old Trolley Rd.
Summerville, SC 29485

www.ChristianPublish.com

Cover Design by Jay Cookingham

Printed in the United States of America and the United Kingdom

Table of Contents

Prologue..5
What is Normal Anyway? 9
God? Where are You?..13
Denial..17
Dancing Across my Battlefield 27
Too Soon to Surrender..33
Drawing Up Our Battle Plans...47
That's Gonna Leave a Mark..55
What if We Lose?..61
Health Care Reform 67
Have No Doubt 71
Fearful Anger 77
Distraction in the Basement..91
God's Timing 99
Five Wishes 103
Shutting the Door to Fear..109
With Us or Against Us..113
Bob's Nadir..119
Unloading Only 129
Heavenly Reinforcements 143
Just a Bump in the Road...151
Please Leave the Radio On...169
Cleft in the Rock 173
Should I Stay or Should I Go?..183
The Garden in the Middle of my Battlefield 189
Using Power of Attorney to Guard My Sacrifice 201
Win - Win Situation 213
Calling Bob Back..219
Super Bowl Seizure...227
Beautiful Urine 237
Home Health...245

Finish the Race 251
Going to Transplant 257
Failed Transplant: I Hate Losing 261
It is Finished 269
Victory in Christ 277
Epilogue 287

Prologue

It's funny how we go through life every day worried about such trivial things. Even those of us who have faith, who claim to know God and trust Him for our every need, still struggle. I'd read the Bible. I believed it, so I thought. This story is about how I came to truly believe, how I fought the good fight of faith. How God held me and my family. He was the only reason we survived, the only reason that we still survive. We battled, we suffered, we picked ourselves up and we battled again.

There are days that I look back at what we went through and wonder how we survived. I look back and see what we went through and how we went through it and wonder how we remained sane. I'm certain that, at times, those around me wondered if I weren't losing my sanity; at times, I wondered the same thing. I was not myself. I was at the end of my rope, hanging on for dear life, mine and my husband's.

There are hard things in this book. I thought very long and hard over whether or not to include everything that I have. There are hard feelings, angry words and thoughts, family division. If it sounds like it is written in battle mode; that is because we were in battle mode. I had to write it in the way I lived it. If I hadn't, there would have been no sense in writing. This is our story.

* * * * * * *

I've seen people stand on stage at church and say, "I've been healed!" I've listened to the crowd clap, cheer and have even seen a few tear drops. However, do we who sit in the crowd really know? No. Unless you've walked it, you do not know the fight that is entailed. I want to share our journey of faith and our road to healing just as it occurred. There were miracles that made us feel like we were on the mountaintop, and there were everyday fights that let us know that we were on the battlefield.

There is a mental, emotional, spiritual battle to fight every day, every minute. The exhaustion of fighting is overwhelming. The fortitude needed to survive this battle is fierce. We had to stand our ground in the face of the enemy. I never knew that simply standing would be so hard.

I hold no bitterness and no offense in my heart. I have since forgiven anyone whom I assumed was out to hurt me. I've asked for forgiveness from those whom I assume I hurt. The relationships that are discussed in this book are mended. It is important that anyone reading this book know that this fight was not against flesh or blood, not against any person or persons. This battle was against cancer, and the enemy was spiritual. The enemy was not a person. Get that! Get that in this book, and get that in your own life. It would be very easy to attach the enemy label to someone whom you perceive is hurting you. Do not get distracted in your fight. The enemy, the spiritual enemy, will throw every distraction at you. Do not be distracted. Stay focused and fight the battle. Fight to win.

So I start this book, knowing that I will journey back through the emotions, through the fear, through the battlefield. But I know it must be written if only for that one person who might be in the midst of his own battle. If but one warrior is on that battlefield praying, begging for help, then I pray that my story may come as part of that help.

I thank Bob's family for staying with us in the fight. I thank them for accepting me into their family, for forgiving me and for loving me.

I thank my family for staying with us in the fight. I thank them for strengthening me, for encouraging me and for loving me.

I thank my church family who reinforced us in our fight. I thank my work family who stayed with us and fought on that battle front. I thank the countless people who encouraged us and cooked for us and did our laundry and cheered us on.

Mostly, I thank the warriors who fought side by side with me. You know who you are. You wear the battle scars proudly.

* * * * * * *

The enemy was Satan. He brought with him cancer and death onto the battlefield that became my life.

Battlefield smoked and charred, I walk through you still. I smell your stench, but it does not permeate, not even the smell of smoke on our clothes as we walk off of this battlefield victorious.

Battlefield, you are larger than I thought you to be. In walking from one side to the other, you have taken a large portion of our lives. I still skirt your borders. I look back over my shoulder and see that you are still there. Our swords are sheathed now, swords that once flew freely, persistently, unashamedly, boldly; always toe-to-toe with our enemy.

My shield of faith that extinguished the enemy's flaming arrows is still hanging from my arm. I have learned to never let this shield go. Warriors who stood beside me held their shields over me at times when I was too weak to lift my own. Now those shields are lifted in victory.

The enemy was cancer, death, the power of darkness. We carried the light through the dark battlefield. We spoke the truth. The truth that we knew was God.

1
What is Normal Anyway?

In the beginning, we were like any other normal family. Bob and I were happily married with two normal teenage daughters, Aimie and Katie. We lived a normal life in Littleton, CO. We went to work Monday through Friday and to church every Sunday. We dealt with the same ups and downs as any other normal family. This story is about how all of that normalcy left.

Back to the beginning. I grew up in the Midwest, part of a normal family. I went to college, graduated with a nursing degree and began to practice as an oncology nurse. Bob grew up in the Midwest also, part of another normal family. Bob graduated from college and moved to Los Angeles to pursue his dream of becoming a Hollywood stuntman. We met in California, moved back to the Midwest, were married, and started our life together. In St. Louis I worked at a cancer center, and Bob worked as an independent contractor. Life was normal. We raised kids, worked, and enjoyed life. In 1996, we moved to Colorado and started our own demolition company. Life was good. I was happy to get away from cancer and death.

In line with leading a normal, good life, we took a beach vacation in the summer of 2003. Bob didn't feel well most of the week; he was tired and had a pounding headache. Upon returning home, he made an appointment with our doctor. The diagnosis was high blood pressure, high enough that our doctor prescribed medication. This was very weird because Bob was a very healthy man. He played soccer three to five times per week, worked physically, worked out, and was in overall great shape. High blood pressure was strange, but manageable. We could deal with this. Over the next month, he went back to the doctor every week to regulate the hypertensive medication.

At one visit, a nurse practitioner not only assessed his blood pressure, energy level and general well-being, but she also ordered blood work and a urine test. This was very fortunate because that urine test started us on a journey that eventually diagnosed Bob. The urine analysis showed large amounts of blood and protein in Bob's urine. The doctor sent us to a specialist. This was the first of many medical specialists whose appointments would soon fill our year. We made an appointment with a urologist. He confirmed the findings and ordered a kidney ultrasound which showed that Bob's kidneys were anatomically normal. He then sent us to a nephrologist, a kidney specialist. I vaguely remember thinking that blood and protein in urine equals bad news. Then, I would tell myself, "He's a normal healthy guy. He's not sick."

We made the appointment with the nephrologist, Dr. Paul. I was so convinced that Bob wasn't sick, I didn't even go to the first appointment with him. I was out of town with the girls at a wedding, and he called.

He said, "Kim, this doctor wants to talk to you a minute."

The doctor asked what tests Bob had already had performed. I told him, and he said that he would draw more blood. I went back to my normal life.

The next week Dr. Paul called me at work to tell me the results of Bob's blood tests. They were all normal, but he wanted to schedule him for a kidney biopsy. Biopsy? Biopsy?! Biopsies look for cancer. Even with my background in oncology, I never connected any test or result he had with cancer. Cancer didn't fit.

We were a normal family, doing normal things; we went to church on Sunday— knew God even! I had a relationship with God. I knew Jesus as my Lord and Savior. I had many, many reasons, proof even, that He existed. He was real to me. I'd experienced miraculous events in my life that solidified my concrete belief in Him and His power. I had started consistently reading my bible and attending a bible-based church twelve years earlier. I had started living my life as I thought God wanted me to, and I had experienced His presence not only in the highs and lows of life, but in my every day life.

Knowing God as I did, I thought, "He can't let this happen to us." I was convinced that it wasn't happening. This was just a bump in the road. We'd figure this out, get past it. We'd have the biopsy, find out he was okay, and get back to our normal life.

My prayers during this first month of tests to diagnose Bob were always the same, always questioning God. That's it. Not very eloquent, but truly gut-wrenching prayers.

"God? What's happening? Tell me!"

Never an answer.

I kept praying, kept asking. Through the few months of tests and blood work, doctors and hospitals, my prayer remained.

"God? Let me know you're here. Please tell me it's going to be okay. Please comfort me with that feeling of 'It'll be okay'."

Nothing. I felt such a void, such emptiness. It was like I was falling, constantly falling, never hitting bottom.

I kept telling God, "I trust You. No matter what, I trust You."

I said that a lot, but I just don't know that I completely believed it at that time. Still, I said it, over and over. "I trust You, God (I hope You know what You're doing.). I trust You, God (Do You know what You're doing?). I trust You, God (God? What are You doing here?)."

2
God? Where are You?

The kidney biopsy was probably a sign of what was to come, as Bob had a complication. Through the next year, we endured many complications. The biopsy was supposed to be an outpatient procedure, but Bob bled from the procedure. Before I really knew exactly what was happening, the nurses were crowding around us and a surgeon was asking me to sign a consent form for a procedure to determine if Bob's renal artery had been nicked. Oh, and just in case, they wanted me to sign this other consent for a possible nephrectomy. It would only be in the worst-case scenario, in case the artery had been cut and couldn't be repaired. It was highly unlikely, but they wanted me to sign it just to be safe. I numbly signed the papers as Bob was being prepped for the procedure. Everything was happening very quickly. The nurses looked extremely nervous.

Bob grabbed my hand and told me, "Kim, just in case anything happens to me, I want you to know that I've been saving some money for us. It's hidden…"

"Stop!" I heard myself yell rather angrily. "Don't you think that way. Nothing is going to happen to you. When you close your eyes, just picture Jesus. He'll take care of you. Okay?" It's the only thing that I knew to say to him.

"Okay, but Kim…"

"NO!" I insisted. I held his hand as they wheeled his stretcher up to a set of double doors.

The doctor told me, "You'll have to wait outside now," and I let go of Bob's hand.

"Pray, Bob!" I ordered him.

One of the nurses directed me to wait in a small waiting room containing six chairs and one table. There was an elderly woman already waiting. She was working on a cross-stitch. She asked if I were okay. I told her about Bob. She was waiting for her husband also. He was having a procedure. She was a retired nurse and now was her husband's care taker, and he had been ill for quite some time. I thought, "I don't want to be Bob's nurse, I want to be his wife."

I asked her husband's name and told her that I would pray for him. She thanked me and told me that prayer was a big part of her life. She told me, "Pray always." I assured her that I would.

Bob's parents were in town visiting their boys, all three of whom live in Colorado, and I called them to tell them that Bob had a complication and was in another procedure. It didn't take them long to get to the hospital. Bob's mother came into the waiting room and sat with us. She was as nervous as I was.

It seemed that we waited forever. I couldn't sit still any longer, and I needed someone to tell me that everything was going to be okay, so I decided to call my mom. She still lived in St. Louis. There was no cell phone reception in the waiting room, so I went outside the nearest door. While I spoke to my mom, I paced back and forth across the parking lot. Upon turning back toward the door on one of my paces, I noticed the doctor who had performed the biopsy running out of the door. I ran to meet him while hanging up the phone with my mom.

"It's venous! He's going to be fine! He doesn't need surgery!" The doctor sounded as excited as I was nervous.

Bob stayed in the hospital for three days and passed approximately twelve blood clots. The bleeding from the procedure was not life-threatening, but the blood would have to come out through his urethra. He passed them like kidney stones.

I've never, to this day, seen him in so much pain.

As fiercely as the pain gripped him, the fear of what was happening was gripping me. I could start to feel its fingers wrapping around me, entangling me. Fear so real that at times I couldn't breath. The results of this biopsy were coming. I'd gone through every possible scenario in my head. I'd have Bob dead and buried one minute and suffering only a weird infection curable by a course of antibiotics the next.

His family spent much of their time over the next three days with us at the hospital, waiting and worrying. Everyone had an opinion, and everyone had questions that couldn't be answered. Everyone was scared. I felt claustrophobic. I was not only being suffocated with my own fear and doubt, but now I had theirs to contend with, too. The questions that they asked seemed to be like weights around my neck.

"Could this be kidney cancer? Could this be some sort of poisoning? Could this be from his diet, his work, his genetics? Should we call another doctor? When will we know? Why can't they tell us anything? What do you think it is? How can we get the answers?"

All valid questions, all questions that I had asked myself. But I had no answers, and I felt as if everyone were looking to me to find them. I didn't really know if I wanted the answer yet. I didn't know if I could handle it yet. Somewhere in me, in my coping, I was still trying to deny that my husband was sick. Bob's family and I were all together in one thing: We were preparing to take a journey together, a journey with no direction.

3
Denial

One month in, and I was already so scared, trying desperately to hold on to denial. I kept thinking of getting him out of there and back to work, back to our normal life. The girls were getting ready to go back to school. Aimie was going away to her first year of college. Katie was going to be a sophomore in high school. We still hadn't finished a few projects around the house that we'd been planning. Life kept going on around us. I was still living my normal life, and this bump in the road was beginning to annoy me. I didn't have time for it. I couldn't let disease steal our normal life. I was grabbing denial with both hands, and I knew it.

A very peculiar thing happened when Bob was in that hospital. An insurance agent called our house one evening, wanting to sell us life insurance. I politely told him that we were already insured. That call placed a thought in my head, though: "When was the last time I received something from my life insurance agent?" Bob and I had purchased a full package of health, life, and disability insurance when we first moved to Colorado. Our agent sent the life insurance invoices yearly. The phone call that I'd received from this new agent while Bob was in the hospital made me question when the last bill was paid. I knew we only received our invoices once per year, but it seemed like it had been longer. I decided that I would check into it after Bob returned from the hospital.

Though denial was the guiding emotion during the first few months of Bob's diagnosis, this call from the life insurance agent planted a new seed in me, the seed of fear. Amidst the denial, I still knew enough about what was happening to Bob to know that something was wrong. Denial allowed me to ignore what was happening. Fear was telling me to prepare for the worst. How could I prepare for the worst yet expect the best? Denial was being pushed out by fear. I searched my office for our life insurance policies. We had not been sent an invoice in approximately thirty months. We had missed two premiums; our policy had lapsed! Now fear completely took over. My plan of preparing for the worst just went down the tubes. How would I maintain our life without a life insurance policy? We had paid five years of premiums for nothing. I tried calling our agent. He had left the company approximately three years earlier and apparently didn't deem it important enough to pass us on to another agent. I realize that I should have known that I hadn't made a payment in almost three years. I decided to call the insurance underwriter and see if we could just pay the delinquent premiums and catch up. They would send us a questionnaire, and once we had completed it, they would re-instate us.

  The agent from the new company (the one who called our house one evening and started me on this hunt) called again and set up an appointment at his office. He assured us that he could do something to help. When he interviewed us, he determined that Bob would not qualify for life insurance at the present time. He tried to get me to sign up for life insurance regardless. I told him, "No." The visit became so unbelievably uncomfortable I thought I was going to break down. I did not want to cry in front of this insurance agent who cared nothing about what was happening in our lives; he just wanted to make a sale. He tried to convince me to sign up for my policy and said that he could wait until Bob was finished with "Whatever this is that he's going through," and if it turned out to be nothing, he would write Bob a policy later.

"There's no reason for you to be irresponsible and not have life insurance just because your husband doesn't qualify."

Was he trying to be helpful or was he really that desperate? All I could hear him saying was, "Your husband is dying."

His quick dismissal of granting Bob a life insurance policy was to me his quick dismissal of worth to Bob's life. After all, aren't the insurance companies just betting we'll live? They didn't think Bob was a safe bet. I did. I was trying to believe that life was going to go back to normal soon; that is what I was betting on. I did not want to listen to a man who didn't even know us tell us that statistically Bob's life wasn't worth betting on. I was appalled. I rose from my chair and told him thanks, but no thanks, and that we'd call him if we needed him. I had no intention of ever calling him again. There was a hint of hope, of faith rising up in me. Denial made me forget what was happening, but now that this insurance agent was taunting us by saying that Bob's death was imminent, I would not lie down to denial any longer. I stood up to this agent, to this enemy of Bob's life.

"You have no idea what we're 'going through'. And you do not know us. We are people of faith; we believe God's word. We are going to walk through this just fine; we don't need your insurance." I was raising my voice to the enemy, not to this insurance agent. I left his office with a feeling of empowerment. There was a fight rising up in me.

Soon enough, the last remnants of denial would slip through my fingers. Try as I might, I couldn't hold on to it any longer. Near the end of August, the nephrologist called with the results of the biopsy. The doctor said he needed a bone marrow biopsy.

I could hear myself speaking over my beating heart, "Why does he need a bone marrow biopsy?" The oncology nurse in me was hiding somewhere.

"We think the proteins are coming from cells in his bone marrow. I am referring him to a cancer center."

"I don't understand."

But I understand. I had treated patients with this disease. I completely understood what was happening on a weird medical, intellectual level. But that me, the oncology nurse, was not there. I was Bob's wife, fearing the loss of my normal life with my normal husband. It was slipping away quickly. In that instant, in that conversation, my denial, my friend, was leaving me. *Bone marrow biopsy... cancer center... proteins... cancer.* It was all running together in my mind, like a movie in fast motion. Quickly, my mind got a handle on what was happening: Bob had cancer. Just as quickly I let that thought go, as if it were too hot, too painful to hold on to. I dropped that thought for fear it would hurt me.

"Wait!" I thought. "Maybe I can still deny this. I can figure this out. I can explain this away."

"God?! God?! Why are you being so quiet?"

God was silent, but it seemed like the devil was jumping up and down in front of me yelling, "Cancer! Cancer! Cancer!"

So just for a brief moment my life, my normal life, crashed down around me, then my subconscious surfaced with, "No! I can't handle this."

So I didn't. I'd wait until we got the results from the bone marrow biopsy. It could still be something else. Denial was back, comforting me into oblivion.

I made the appropriate phone calls, told our family members, "We still don't have a diagnosis. The doctors want to run more tests at a cancer center and do a bone marrow biopsy." There, that was easy. Somewhere in me, I knew it was cancer, but I couldn't wrap my mind around that yet. I kept it inside of me where it would be safely hidden. If I didn't tell anyone, it wasn't really happening, right?

I had given both his family and my family all of the information that Bob and I had received. We gave them all that we knew for sure, which was essentially nothing. More tests meant that we still knew nothing for sure. Unfortunately, I knew. I knew what was happening.

The one person that I couldn't keep the truth from was my mom. Not because she was a nurse, too, and knew what a bone marrow biopsy was, but because she knew me too well. The day I told her about the ensuing visit to the cancer center and scheduled bone marrow biopsy is like a blur to me. I can remember some of the strangest details about the conversation yet not remember if she called me or I called her. Was it August or September? Had I told anyone else yet? Did I try to convince her, as I'd tried to convince myself, that this could still be just a weird infection? I remember vividly that I was sitting in my car in the driveway. I had just gotten home. It was a beautiful day. I was wearing a blue tee shirt and jeans. I was telling her the latest news and what was to come.

I thought I was holding it together so well and then she said, "Do you need your dad and me to come out there?" They still lived in the Midwest. Dad had retired the previous year, and she had just retired that week.

I said, "I don't know."

I did know that I needed help. I didn't know how to ask because I was afraid to ask. I couldn't tell her I needed them, as I was still trying to ride that wave of denial. How could I lose it now? I couldn't. I had to stay in control.

Then she said, in a very calm voice that I can still hear today, "All you need to do is tell us when, and we'll come."

That did it. I lost it. I was so confused. I wanted to be the little girl again who cried out to her parents, "Help me!", yet I was still the woman who kept telling herself that everything was going to be okay. My answer was somewhere in between.

"How do I know when I need you, Mom? I'm already so scared; I don't know what to do! I don't know that you and Dad can help. I don't know what you can do; I don't even know what I'm doing! I don't know if I need you yet. How will I know?"

I sobbed, laid my head down on my steering wheel, and cried so hard that I cried my contacts out of my eyes.

My mom said, "We're coming." I don't remember hanging up. I don't remember the date of their move; I just know they came. They moved to Colorado. They left the first house they'd ever owned, the house that they raised all six of their children in. They left their peers, brothers, sisters, nieces, nephews, and neighbors of thirty-six years, at the drop of a hat. We needed them, and that's all they needed to know. They came. I was in such a funk over everything that was happening that I didn't even comprehend the weight of what they had done until about a year later, when I asked my mom, "When did you move here?"

She replied, "I had just retired. Bob was sick. I asked if you needed us, and you fell apart. I hung up and told your dad, 'We're moving to Colorado'."

Easy as that. Thank You, God, for giving her ears to hear.

Bob and I continued to make every attempt to keep our normal life. We made the appointment for the bone marrow biopsy at the cancer center but went back to life. Bob worked just as hard as ever, trying to make up for the lost time that he'd spent in doctors' offices.

The girls started school. My sister Paula and I took Aimie to college. We helped her move into her first dorm room. Paula is not a woman to show much emotion. She's very rational, very solid, very logical, a lot like Bob, but as we left Aimie, she wept. I couldn't allow myself to cry. I wouldn't; I was just trying to keep myself together.

Dropping Aimie off at college to start her new life was a very normal thing to do. This was just part of life. It seemed like a happy thing to do. I hadn't told Aimie any real news about Bob yet. How could I? This was her first year of college. How could I start that life off with news of death, of cancer? I couldn't. Besides, we didn't even really know if it was truly cancer yet, right?

Katie started school, too. This would be her first year of being the only child at home. She missed Aimie horribly. Everything around her was changing. She could feel it. A few months into the semester, she wrote a paper entitled *Life Goes On* about feeling that her sister leaving was one of the saddest events of her life until she found out that her dad had cancer. She grew up a lot that year. It wasn't fair.

We soon received the questionnaire in the mail from our original life insurance policy underwriter. It was a quick one-page form with a letter stating that we could just answer the questions and start paying again, and that there would be no physical. They would simply reinstate our policy. No problem, except the one-page questionnaire asked if either of us were presently under a doctor's care. It also asked if either one of us had been diagnosed with high blood pressure, kidney disease, or cancer. Bob and I held onto that questionnaire for what seemed like an eternity. Those were the only questions that held us back. We could lie. We could just complete the form and send it in with a check. After all, it wasn't our fault that we had missed payments, right? We did not intentionally drop our life insurance. They're the ones who didn't send us the bill. Bob wasn't really diagnosed with anything yet, either. It would not be completely dishonest. We had every excuse ready for the deception that we could have enacted. The problem was that Bob and I were honest people. It was hard for us, as honest people, to be dishonest. We never sent the questionnaire back. We were getting ready to walk this journey, to dance this dance with death, without life insurance. We knew what we were doing. We were betting on life.

 Some days I was haunted by the questionnaire that still sat incomplete in a file. Something drew me to it. Was it fear? For weeks I danced with this fear. I would doubt my resolve to be an honest person and consider filling it out just to see if we'd be re-instated. I would consider calling an attorney and demanding that we be re-instated with or without the questionnaire. Then I would argue with myself saying that I was showing a lack of faith by wanting to re-instate. I was betting on life, remember? Weirdly enough, I had convinced myself that if I pushed for the life insurance to be re-instated, I was betting on the fact that Bob wasn't going to make it. I would then be bowing to the fear. If I could stand on faith and believe in God, I wouldn't need the insurance companies. God would take care of me either way. I would only bow to

God. The dance continued but with new partners. I never danced with the life insurance issue again. However, my new dance partners were just as pushy.

4
Dancing Across my Battlefield

Some people wait almost a year to get a final diagnosis. Sometimes doctors run tests and more tests and refer patients to specialists and more specialists and finally they're diagnosed. For Bob and me, it was two months from, "I have a headache" to, "You have bone marrow cancer." The comfort of denial only lasted two months. Then I couldn't be comforted by it any longer.

In the middle of September 2003, our new doctor, a hematologist at the cancer center near our home, gave us the results from the bone marrow biopsy. As he drew pictures and explained how normal bone marrow produces blood cells, I watched as if I'd never seen anything like it before. It was as if he were teaching us something of which I had a vague recollection in a distant past.

It looked so familiar and yet brand new. Plasma cells – huh? Myeloma? He gave us pamphlets and literature on bone marrow cancer. As I held the papers in my hands, I looked down at the word "myeloma." I repeated it in my head over and over. Myeloma. Myeloma. Myeloma. I tried to remember patients from my past whom I had treated for the disease. I didn't want to remember, but I couldn't block them out. They were all middle-aged, and they had all lost their battle with cancer. I took the pamphlets, the papers with the pictures that the doctor had drawn, and the latest yellow lab result sheet and shoved them in my purse.

How was I going to deny this now? God?!

I just decided not to dwell on the cancer. The doctor had told us it was a very atypical presentation, so maybe he was wrong. Maybe it wasn't myeloma after all. I tried so hard to keep denying. I knew in my gut that he had cancer, but I couldn't let myself completely buy into it yet. I just wasn't ready.

My new dance partner was showing himself. Cancer. It was actually always the same partner, though, really just disguised for different parts of the dance. It was death that we danced with. Always death.

****

It is strange that as I write this, I look back at the difference between dancing and fighting. When I let my unwelcome partner lead, it was a dance. When I stood up and consciously refused his advances, refused to allow him to move me in the direction that he desired, I turned his dance into a fight. We danced and fought across a battlefield for years. In those years I found my weapon and my battle dress, my arsenal: the sword of the word, the shield of faith, the belt of truth, the breastplate of righteousness, the helmet of salvation, the shoes of readiness. My strength was found on that battlefield, in that battle and in that dance.

Instead of allowing myself to fall apart or to fall into the arms of this dance partner, I consciously decided to fight. I was not going to take it. I was going to figure out how we were going to beat this enemy. I wouldn't listen to the doctors when they told us that the disease was not curable. They said it often: no cure. Instead of listening to that nonsense, I began to plan. It was like drawing up a battle plan. I threw myself completely on God and began to journal every emotion. I had started a journal in 1992, at the urging of my best friend's mother, I wrote frequently at times, I would skip blocks of months at other times. My relationship with God was loosely journaled over the past eleven years.

When Bob was being diagnosed, I began to journal daily! I wrote everything down on paper. I'd read my fear, read my anxiety, and then attack it. As fiercely as the enemy was attacking me and my family, I'd fight back, on paper. I'd read my feelings and then change them, correct them with the word of God.

One passage from my journal dated September 16, 2003 reads:

> *Jesus, be my Prince of Peace. Biopsy results show atypical myeloma. We found out yesterday. Rejoice in the Lord always, again I say rejoice! Thank Him; praise Him. Rejoice in the Lord always. I don't like this. I don't even feel like I know how to pray right now. I feel weak. I don't know if I'm doing what I'm supposed to do, or even if I'm where I'm supposed to be. I can feel my heart pounding; my chest hurts. I can't follow a thought. I don't know how to tell Aimie and Katie. Oh, Father, protect them. Please, God, hold them in Your hands and love them today. Let them feel Your love, Your mercy. Help to open their eyes today to how awesome You are. Speak to them, Father, so that they may hear You. Speak to me, too. I need You, God, more than ever before. I'm here—speak. You might have to speak loudly. I'm not hearing very well right now.*

Instead of praying, "God? Where are you?" like a lost child full of fear and looking to her Father for answers, in disbelief that she is lost, I would start looking in the Bible for verses to pray, for verses to hold on to. As strongly as I had previously held on to denial, I would now begin to hold on to the word of God. As long as I denied that Bob had cancer, the farther away from the truth I ran, the farther away from God I felt.

Lost.

God? I was asking where He was, but He hadn't moved. I had. I was backing away, so afraid to face what was ahead yet knowing what was there, knowing we'd have to go through it. I was the one backing away, but not anymore. I knew God, remember? I knew from my past that God was able to do more than we could ask or even imagine. I would not pray, "God? Where are you? What's going on?" anymore. I knew what was going on. I was starting a battle with the enemy. The enemy was Satan, and he was trying to kill my husband. I prepared for battle!

* * * * * * *

I started in Psalms. I would read my journal and write verses that spoke to me. I cried to God, poured my heart out to Him, poured myself out to Him. I begged Him to show me how to live, how to fight this enemy. Forget normalcy. What is normal, anyway? I read and prayed and cried to God every morning, every night. I told Him every thought, every fear. I gave it all to Him. It was safe there. I stopped denying that cancer, the enemy, was there, and I turned to face it. I would not back up—I would stand my ground. Life continued, but now it was intertwined with death. I could feel death, cancer, the enemy, hovering. The dance had turned into a fight. The battle had begun.

Something about knowing and accepting what was happening was weirdly invigorating. I could take action. I could stay busy. I felt, no, *knew* that I had to prepare. I knew the Bible held the answers to every question. I knew that God would speak to me, so I ravaged His word. I'd pour my feelings onto the pages of my journal, so many times writing through the tears that fell into the paper faster than the words. I'd find something in the Bible to correlate to how I was feeling. I was confident that God knew my fears and was counting up my tears. Just knowing that He was there made it more bearable. I'd ask God, "How are we going to do this?" I'd find stories about men and women who had suffered great trials and wonder, "How did they do it?" I was filling myself with faith, encouraging myself with the word of God. It was working!

The Bible says that in order to come boldly before God, to present my needs to Him, I needed to cleanse myself of sin. I knew I needed to be near him so I prayed.

On September 18, 2003, I wrote the following:

The disease is nothing when You are near, God. Be near! I need to hear You, to feel You, God. Please God, comfort us. I love You. Forgive us our sins. Forgive me, Father, for my sins. Cleanse me. Help me to forgive those who have sinned against me. I praise You, God; I worship You, Father. I fear Your judgment. Jesus, stand in the gap. Lord Jesus, hear and protect us. Save us, Jesus, save us. Protect us from the enemy. Fill me with Your Spirit again, make me new and fresh. Forgive me first, Lord, forgive me for questioning You, for questioning myself. Forgive me, take me back into Your sweet presence. I'm sorry, God, I want to stand before You with only love and forgiveness in my heart. I need to be near You now, God. I need ushered in by Your Spirit. Lead me, Father.

O God, do not keep silent, be not quiet, O God, be not still.

I am forgiven, I am made whole. I am healed and made one with Him. "Eat of my flesh," He said, "Drink of My blood." I have, and I will, I will know Him, and He will know me. God is forever with me, never, never, leaving me. I turn to Him completely. He is mine, and I am His. Thank You, God. Thank You, Jesus. Praise, Glory, and Honor to You. Watch me, keep me. I love You. I need You.

I was convincing myself that we would fight this battle, win (because God was on our side), and move on. Sounds easy, right? I had no clue of what we were up against. I said many times over the next year to never underestimate the power of the enemy. He is a worthy and evil adversary. Without God, without faith, we would have been squelched in an instant. Our power, our might is nothing. Without the spirit of the Lord, we would have never made it. Maybe it was good that we had no idea of what was to come. We walked by blind faith onto the battlefield.

5
Too Soon to Surrender

Due to the fact that the presentation of myeloma was so atypical, the hematologist had encouraged us to go to the Mayo Clinic to visit yet another specialist for a more definitive diagnosis and treatment options. He told us that this Mayo Clinic specialist was the best in the country and that he had literally written the book that other doctors read and learn from on myeloma. Because of the strange presentation in Bob, he'd like treatment courses to be determined by this Mayo guru. He said, "It'll be the best $5,000 you'll ever spend." I think he hadn't dealt with insurance out-of-network co-payments, airfare, and hotels often. It was actually $11,000, and I could have thought of a lot of better ways to spend it. The first week of October 2003, while our kids settled into new school years, we settled into our battle positions and headed off to Rochester, MN, the home of the world-renowned Mayo Clinic.

The Mayo Clinic is a place that has inspired both awe and hate in me. The nurse in me was starting to return, and that part of me was amazed at how well this huge institution operated. It was utterly amazing, like being in a health museum that was filled with health care professionals all at the top of their game. We checked into our hotel room. We'd be there one week. We decided to pretend that we were on vacation. Never mind that no one in his right mind would take an $11,000 vacation in Rochester, MN; however we were determined to make the best of this trip.

Since we were doing this trip vacation-style, our first order of business was to find a nicer hotel that the one I had booked online. It just wasn't going to do, so we checked out the area and found a suite at the Radisson that was much more vacation-oriented. If we were going to spend a week there, we at least needed room to move around in, a table and chairs, a couch, a few movie channels, and of course, room service. There was also a Plaza Club that we had access to. We used our key to access an upstairs banquet room that provided free breakfast, happy hour food and beverages, and bed-time snacks. It was starting to sound more like vacation.

The morning of our appointment, we walked across the pedestrian bridge to the Mayo Building and found our way to the lobby to sign in at the receptionist's window. The registration area reminded me of a large bank lobby with a row of approximately twenty teller windows. What did I expect? This *was* the Mayo Clinic. Bob was called to window fourteen, so we approached a very nice but very business-like woman. She issued him a clinic number, a number he would have forever, so if he'd ever come back, he'd already be registered. He was number six million and something.

My mind said, "Wow, amazing record keeping organization." My gut said, "We're not coming back; keep your number."

She gave Bob his registration folder and directed us to our first appointment, pointing over our shoulders and saying, "You go to the first bank of elevators, through the marble lobby, past the man playing the grand piano, and under the hanging blown glass art work to the West Mayo Building. Choose one of the six sets of elevators up to the tenth floor. Go to ten West and sign in at the desk. Thank you, and good luck." I smiled. We didn't need luck; we had faith.

We followed her directions, made it to the desk, signed in and waited for the woman behind the desk to say something. "Thank you. Take a seat."

That's it? Take a seat? That's all? We flew all of the way from Denver, checked into a hotel, navigated our way to the office and we get, "Take a seat."!? I expected back handsprings, fireworks, something, but we got, "Take a seat." I felt like screaming; instead we sat.

We chose our seat from the one-hundred and thirty-five chairs that were in the waiting room. Yes, one-hundred and thirty-five. I counted them. Nervous, heart beating a mile-a-minute, I counted the chairs. I needed to have something for my mind to do. I had just finished with the chairs and was starting on the ceiling tiles when a nurse came out from behind a set of double doors, grabbed a microphone and called, "Mr. Hritz." We were going in.

The hallway that led to the exam room was old, wide, and clean. We walked on burnt orange colored 9"x 9" floor tiles, down the hall to the exam room. The exam room had an old wooden antique-looking exam table. It was beautiful. The room also held a couch, a dressing room, a chair, a desk, and a scale. We waited.

The guru's associate doctor, or Fellow, came in to perform a history and physical. He was very nice and very thorough. He was very normal, nothing Mayo-esque about him. I'm not really sure what I was expecting. We described in detail the past two and a half months of our lives. It sounded so clinical. The fellow left and said he would return shortly with Dr. McAdams, "The myeloma guru." They returned almost immediately and spent approximately two minutes with us.

"We'd like to get some more tests to better determine your diagnosis; we'll meet again Wednesday. Stop at the front desk for your schedule."

Schedule? We stopped at the front desk and questioned the woman about this schedule. She handed us a four-page syllabus. It contained a schedule for the week, with pre-test and post-test instructions and directions to each testing area. It also listed the tests: blood, urine, another bone marrow biopsy, fat aspiration biopsy, EKG…wow! First to the Hilton Building desk C-1 (see map enclosed), next to the Guggenheim Building at noon, drop urine specimen cup in the bag provided, then brown bag it and place it in one of the "S drop boxes" located around the Mayo facility, nothing to eat after midnight…etc., etc., etc.

Did anyone realize how overwhelmed we were?

I read the schedule as we walked back to our room. Yes, it was back to our vacation now. We walked through the facility, past the Gap store, the bagel shop, coffee shops, shoe stores, jewelry stores, and thought that maybe we could do a little vacationing here. We had the whole evening to kill before heading back in the morning for more testing. We went upstairs to try out our Plaza Club Lounge. We met Sharon, a nice young woman who was working the happy hour. We ate free appetizers, fresh pineapple and chicken quesadillas, as we watched the room fill up. Sharon spoke to everyone. Some customers, patients of Mayo Clinic all, were regulars; some, like us, were new to all of this. Sharon's casual conversation came to mean a lot to us that week. We were out of our element, scared and confused. We were meeting lab technicians, nurses, doctors all week, and then there was Sharon. We began to associate with her familiarity. In that week at the Radisson, we didn't miss an evening of happy hour or night-time milk and cookies. It was our one bit of routine that managed to keep us sane.

During the days at the Mayo Clinic, I went into auto-pilot of sorts. I took control of getting us to the right building, the right testing area. I asked the nurses and lab technicians for the results to every test and questioned everything that they were doing. I was Bob's personal private duty nurse. I took control of his care. I was doing everything I could to stay strong for him. At night, back in our room, I fell apart.

On our second night there, I wrote in my journal:

We're at the Mayo Clinic. I don't want to be the strong one. I don't want to be the one in charge. I want him to take care of me. I want my husband to be stronger than I am. I want him back! I don't want to take care of him; I don't want to have to answer all of his questions. Why doesn't he understand? I love him so much. I want him back. I want him to be my Bob again. Will he ever? Will I still love him if he's not? Yes, of course I will. This city is full of sick people. Not us, we're not sick. I hate this place. I hate the Mayo Clinic. People depending on doctors to fix them. Who can make them better? I hate this! Tests, more biopsies, I hate this! I hate the Mayo Clinic!!

On October 8, we met with Dr. McAdams again. One little visit with this calm, pleasant man began to define what our immediate future would be. We were thrown into a world of chaos. Bob's official diagnosis was Kappa Light Chain Deposition Disease—Randall type. It was rare. It was probably diagnosed as myeloma by many doctors. He said that he saw about twelve cases per year. There was not a lot of data to support a "choice" treatment due to the low number of cases studied. In Bob's case we would need to watch his kidney function closely and base treatment on how well his kidneys could tolerate whatever we chose. The disease was not curable.

We weren't looking for a cure: We were going to be healed!

Bob's kidney function was already, by his account, at only 75%. The disease was currently affecting his kidneys. If we had no treatment at all, Bob's renal insufficiency would progress to end-stage renal failure. He would need to go on dialysis. That was not an option. As he listed the possible treatment options, my mind began to grasp the familiarity of what he was saying. "Oral chemotherapy, steroids, bone marrow transplant..." Oh, my God! Bob has cancer! Why was it still taking so long to sink in!?

As he continued to discuss treatment options, none of which I was ready to accept yet, I heard Bob say, "Am I going to be able to work? We own a business. I have people who work for me; they depend on me. How long will all of this take? How much will it cost?" and so Bob began to realize what was happening. Life was changing.

Dr. McAdams said he would set up a consult with a bone marrow transplant doctor at Mayo, and he'd try to get us in on Friday. "But we're going back home Friday," Bob said.

"I think you should see this doctor first," Dr. McAdams replied. "You can speak to a social worker and an insurance specialist, too." He continued talking like we were going to stay there! No!

"We're going to have to think about all of this," I said. "We're not ready to make any decisions right now. We're a little freaked out."

"I understand. We'll get the bone marrow consult set up for Friday and go from there. I'm sorry."

The visit ended. We checked out, received our next appointment time and map and left. We held hands as we started the walk back to our room. We tried to figure out how to tell the girls. Bob didn't want to talk to anyone. We decided that I would make the phone calls. That afternoon on our walk back from the doctor's office, we stopped at a GAP. I bought a pair of pants and a shirt. Next, we stopped at a shoe store. I had noticed a pair of red shoes in the window, and Bob convinced me to go in and try them on. Bob and I both tried on shoes. The man who was helping us asked if we were there for the clinic. Wasn't everyone, I thought?

"Yes, my husband is sick." Oh, my gosh! I said it out loud, to a stranger! I was trying on talking about this disease like I was trying on that pair of red shoes. Neither fit. The man explained how he had been diagnosed years ago with an eye disorder that he sought treatment for here at Mayo. He eventually came so much that he decided to move here.

NOOOO!!!!!! Everything in me screamed. Why? Why move your life to follow a doctor, a clinic? Why move your life to camp next to death?? NO! I listened to Bob explain the disease that was threatening us, explaining our enemy, to this man. They talked about all of the patients who had passed through. This man had met a lot of them. I hurried Bob along. I found the appropriate size shoes, Bob found some too. We bought our shoes and left.

Once back in our room, I made the phone calls. I called my mom first. I could tell by her voice that she was worried. I imagine that I recounted what the doctor had said, but I honestly don't remember the conversation. I only remember that it was brief, and by the end of it, she had assumed a role that she'd taken very often in my life: very authoritative, very strong, and very in-control.

"Kim, we'll get through this. We'll be okay. Pray."

Thanks, Mom.

I vaguely remember calling a few of my brothers and sisters, and my brother Rusty said, "Don't freak out. It could be worse, Kim; we'll get through this. Say a prayer. I'll pray for you."

Thanks, Rusty.

Paula, who also happened to work with us, said, "Should I put an ad in the paper and start hiring? Should I hire an estimator? Should I tell anyone at work? Don't worry, the business will be okay." Paula and Bob being very much alike was made even more obvious to me by the way they both reacted that day: very logically, and very practically.

Bob made me call his parents because he said that he wouldn't be able to talk to them without crying. I told him it was okay to cry, but he didn't want to scare them. They were scared anyway, and they didn't seem to understand.

"Is it cancer?" his mother kept asking. I was in no position to explain in detail what was happening. I was still trying very hard to understand it for myself. I knew I would be of no help comforting anyone else, so the conversations were all very brief. I don't remember what was said in most of them.

The enemy was starting to slap me around a bit, and I had to get my bearings before I could speak. I wanted to choose my words carefully.

After the phone calls, we went up to the Plaza Club for appetizers. We walked in and were the first ones there. Bob checked out the buffet table: chicken skewers, fresh pineapple again, cheese and crackers, and something that I hadn't noticed before, a full bar. As if I hadn't been numbed enough by the day that we'd had, I decided a glass of wine might help. One glass of wine might help me sleep. After all, it had been a heck of a day.

As Sharon poured my complimentary glass of wine, she asked where we were from, the usual small talk. Then the question, "So what are you guys here for?"

"My husband is sick." I'd said it again for the second time in just a few hours. Why was everyone making me say it? She told me about how wonderful the doctors were. I changed the subject.

"Have you lived here all of your life?" I wanted to talk about her life. She obliged. More small talk. That was better. Bob ate, I drank, and we all talked. It was nice. We didn't talk about disease or Mayo. We just talked. One glass of wine led to two then three. When it was time to go back to our room, I was definitely numb enough to sleep, right? Wrong. I spent the first half hour in my room on the phone with my brother Stan in yet another conversation that I don't remember.

He told me later, "You were a mess."

What I do remember about that night is that I went into the bathroom, locked the door, and started to cry. Really cry. I didn't want to break down in front of Bob because I needed to be strong for him. I figured that I'd cry for a bit, pray, and feel okay. It's amazing that I tried to stay so in control I even scheduled my breakdowns.

Well, in the bathroom that night, October 8, 2003, my breakdown could not be controlled. I was ashamed that I felt drunk, then again I felt justified in my rebellion. I was so mad, so very confused. There are no words for the way I felt.

I was petrified, determined, confused. I knew too much about cancer, felt I knew too little, and I was afraid that I was being broken and couldn't figure a way to stop it. I was completely and totally lost and alone. I lay down on the cold hard tile floor and curled up in a ball. I rocked back and forth and repeated over and over, "I can't do this, God. I can't, God; I'm not this strong. Really, it's too much for me to bear. I can't do this, God; I can't." I yelled at God, as if the volume of my voice would grab His attention and make Him listen.

****

The Bible says that we all have our cross to bear. Before Jesus carried His cross, He went to a garden, the garden of Gethsemane, where He cried and asked God to "take this cup" from Him. Eventually Jesus said, "Not My will but Yours be done."

My garden was a bathroom floor in Rochester, MN. I begged God to take this cup from us. I cried, screamed, begged Him. I never got to the "Not my will but Yours be done" part. I had formally lodged my complaint with God. I can't do this; take it away. He didn't. I thought I was being broken. I hadn't broken yet. I left my garden without being broken. I would visit that garden of Gethsemane again. God would be merciful enough to give me another chance to surrender my will.

Eventually, Bob knocked on the door long enough for me to get up and let him in. As soon as I unlocked the door, I retreated back to my position on the floor, rocking back and forth repeating, "I can't do this, I can't." Poor Bob must have thought I had lost it. I can only imagine what this was doing to him. He unlocked my arms from around my knees, stood me up, and allowed me to scream and cry and hit him.

"I can't do this! I'm scared! I don't want you to die! You can't die! You can't leave me! Stop this! Stop it! You don't understand what's happening! A bone marrow transplant! Bob, don't do this! You can't, it's too hard!" Over and over again until he stopped me.

He pulled me in close, wrapped his arms very tightly around me and said, "Shhh. Stop now. It's not you, it's me, and I can handle this. I can do this, Kim. I'll get through it. I'm as tough as they come, and I know I can handle this. Now, shhh."

I appreciated the sentiment, but I knew that he had no idea what he was in store for. The funny thing is that I thought I did. After all, I had taken care of bone marrow transplant patients, so I assumed I knew what was coming. As bad as I imagined it would be wasn't even close to what we actually endured.

We went to bed while Bob continued to hold me. I tried to calm down and catch my breath. My whole world was falling apart. I knew that the arms that I was feeling comfort me would soon not be there. I didn't want to be the strong one; it wasn't fair. He was the man; he was supposed to be the strong one. But I would have no choice: In sickness and in health was a covenant I had made.

****

We called the airlines and changed our return flight so that we could see the BMT specialist Friday morning at Mayo. We asked lots of questions, and he gave some answers. I stared at my new red shoes while he described our options. We could do nothing (not recommended), take oral chemotherapy (not recommended either), take oral steroids in high doses for a four month trial (maybe), or go straight to bone marrow transplant. The goal was to kill the plasma cells that were creating these light chain proteins that were clogging up Bob's kidneys. We talked about the risks and benefits of each treatment in detail. There was no cure (again with this?), but a bone marrow transplant seemed the most promising for longest remission.

"What would you do if it were you?" I asked, looking up from my shoes.

"Ultimately, it's up to you two. I'm not in your shoes, and honestly I don't know if I could answer that question. I'm just trying to give you as much information as I can so that you can make an informed decision." He paused for a moment. We stared at him. "It is truly your decision to make," he stated slowly and deliberately. It was going to be our road to walk, our decision to make, our cross to bear. It didn't seem so at the time, because I just wanted someone to tell us what to do, but that was the best advice we could have gotten.

We told him that we would like a prescription for the high-dose steroids and that Bob would start taking them while we decided what we were going to do. We thanked him and told him that we were going to go home to Colorado now. We now had a definitive diagnosis and appropriate treatment options, so we would pursue treatment at home. We had kids, a business, and a life to get back to. He gave us the prescription for high-dose steroids and told us that he thought we were doing the right thing.

Bob and I went back to our room, packed, and discussed treatment options. We decided that afternoon that since Bob was young and healthy, we would have the bone marrow transplant. We prayed together, cried together, and decided together.

"Let's hit it as hard as we can. I can take it," he said.

I agreed with the hit-it-hard part but was doubting whether or not he could take it. I told him everything to expect, at least everything that I could think of. I explained how hard it would be. I told him about the mouth sores, diarrhea, nausea, vomiting, weakness, blood transfusions, platelet transfusions, no appetite, risk of infection, etc.

"I can do this, Kim," he repeated. I reminded him he'd be out of work for a minimum of six weeks, most likely more than that. Was I trying to prepare him or to convince him to be as scared as I was?

He stayed strong. "Kim, I can do this."

What I said was less comforting, "I don't know if I can." Doubt and fear were always there to fill the void that denial had left.

We returned to Denver to meet the BMT doctor there, prepare, and fight the good fight. It would be hard, but we could do it. Bob's "I can do it" attitude won out, and I was fearfully on board. We called the families and told them that we were going home.

We decided not to go over every detail with each of them on fifteen different phone calls, and instead invited everyone who could make it over to our house for a family get together, planned for the night after we were to arrive home. The phone calls were brief, "Rare bone marrow disease, like myeloma called Kappa Light Chain Deposition Disease. There is no real cure, but lots of treatment options which we will discuss with you all when we get home. Can you please come to our house for coffee and discussion?" After the phone calls, we went up to the Plaza Club, got our nightly milk and freshly baked cookies, brought them back to our room and ordered a movie, Johnny Depp's *Pirates of the*

Caribbean. We were spending the last night of our vacation in Rochester, MN.

The next morning, sitting on the plane, I settled the score in my head. The enemy had struck a few devastating blows, but none were fatal. We could tell we were in the battle, a bit bruised and battered, but okay. We were retreating back to our home to lick our wounds and prepare for the next phase. We'd made it through diagnosis. Bob was sick. We'd accepted it and were ready to fight back. We were preparing mentally for a bone marrow transplant. I knew my enemy. I'd seen people recover from bone marrow transplants before; we could do this. We had a strong family, a strong faith. I even convinced myself that Bob would be able to work from home. I could bring him blue prints, and he could bid jobs. He'd be slower and might have a few weeks that he'd be totally out of commission, but even our business would survive. We had not yet begun to fight.

6
Drawing Up Our Battle Plans

Since Bob and I had gone through so much over the diagnosis process, we had been able to slowly digest what was happening. We were out of denial; we were preparing ourselves for battle. We had been so preoccupied taking care of ourselves that we had ignored how this diagnosis was affecting everyone else. It was so hard to take in this new information, but it was even harder to watch everyone else take it in. I knew that we were collecting information and preparing a plan on how to fight, but I didn't know what anyone else was doing with the information. I honestly could not help anyone else in dealing with it because I was consumed with my own coping and my own strategy-building.

Our girls were as scared as we were but were so wonderfully strong. They, like us, tried to maintain as much normalcy as possible. However, they, like us, knew that normalcy would be on hold for a while. It was so hard to be normal when everyone was trying to invade our space. They immediately fell into the only coping skills that they knew: Prayer. They told me often, "Just keep praying, Mom."

Bob and I arrived home from Mayo. We prepared for our family meeting. We were laying out our battle plan for all to see. His two brothers and their wives came, along with my parents, my brother Stan, and Paula. We had coffee and cookies. Bob had asked me to start since I could explain medically what was happening. So I did. I shared how normal bone marrow worked and what was "abnormal" about Bob's bone marrow. Everyone listened intently. So far so good.

As soon as my anatomy and physiology lesson was over, they started asking questions. How, when, why did this happen? We did not have the answers to everything. What can the doctors do to help? We laid out the treatment options that we had been given and told them that we had decided on a bone marrow transplant. There were questions, most I thought to be somewhat normal, except when Bob's brother asked if we had considered seeing more doctors.

"More doctors?" I asked. "We've seen six already, not to mention the doctors I know and have worked with back in St. Louis. I've already contacted them by phone and email to discuss Bob's diagnosis. We've even been to the Mayo Clinic."

What didn't he understand? We did not want to travel to more doctors just to hear the same thing over again. Bob explained to his brothers that we'd seen enough doctors, and we knew that we wanted the transplant. He didn't want to wait any longer. "I want to get this over with and get back to work," he told Steve.

We were in such a different place than they were. I don't know that we were ever on the same page. After approximately an hour of questions about diagnosis and treatment, the questions turned to suggestions. Everyone seemed to have an opinion of what they thought Bob and I should do.

The consensus among Bob's family seemed to be, "If you're going to have a bone marrow transplant, you should find out where the best place in the country is to have one." There were even offers to help us afford to seek housing in other states, and offers to have family members move with us for the duration of treatment.

"Wait a minute!" Bob finally said, "We're not asking for all of this. We have kids here and a business. We can't move; we're having the transplant here. We're not asking you to make this decision for us; we're really just asking for your support, please. And you guys know how worried Mom and Dad will be, and that they'll try to make us go to a hundred doctors, and they'll try to make decisions for us, too. Can you please just ask them to support us, too? If they start to get nervous, just help them understand that we only want their support."

His brothers agreed: They'd help with his parents and family, and they would support us. The evening went on longer than I wanted it to, but we owed it to them to be able to question us. Everything seemed so clear to us. So why were they all so confused?

The evening finally ended. We had formally presented all the facts to both families and were expecting support for the battle that was to come. If Bob and I had been the generals of this battle and our families were the troops, we would soon find that there was a mutiny brewing.

Though we were aware that everyone had only the best of intentions, and only wanted to help us, Bob and I were not good at accepting help. The more our families pushed to help, the more we resented the offers. It seemed as if the offers for help were a constant reminder that Bob was sick. Everyone seemed to be trying to change our battle plan. They all wanted to decide the direction we should be going, and we had already laid out our plans! It seemed like they were creating more of a fight for us, and we had to fight just to stay focused on our original plan.

Naturally, our families wanted to be a big part of our lives during this time. Because Bob and I had always been so self-sufficient, we felt a bit invaded by all of the new help in our lives. They were there for us, but their presence also felt like constant reminders of the changes that were occurring. I don't mean to sound ungrateful for the help that was offered. We knew that the offers were genuine. We knew that everyone was offering out of love and concern. Unfortunately, the more his family pushed to help us, the more we resisted it. We soon discovered that Bob's family evidently disagreed with our plan of attack, and in pushing their "help" on us, they were trying to re-write our battle plan.

They were feeling helpless and were looking for anything to do to help. In the constantly-expressed sentiment of "We're only trying to help," they began to second guess every single decision that Bob and I had made together. Maybe we hadn't been to the right doctor? Maybe we needed to see someone in Seattle, Texas, St, Louis? Maybe Bob should ask who the best doctor in the country was to treat this disease? Maybe he should try a new drug that they had found on the internet?

They faxed over articles they had read on the disease and testimonials from patients who had been fighting it for years. One particular night as I was cooking spaghetti, Bob read me a fax that his parents had sent. A woman who had suffered with myeloma was explaining how her kidneys had failed and she'd started dialysis; another woman explained how she'd lost her husband to the disease. Bob started to cry.

I pulled the fax from his hand, tore it into pieces, threw it away, and told him, "That's it! You need to tell your family to stop now, or I will. It's time for them to get on board here and do what we asked: Support us!"

He called and told them that the fax was too hard to read and asked if they knew what was in it. They said they'd read it and thought it was encouraging. I had to give Bob an over-the-counter medication to help him get to sleep that night. He just kept saying, "Why are they doing this to me?"

I told him they obviously didn't know that their actions were hurting him; he needed to tell them how he felt. I was certain that they would stop if they knew the harm they were causing. I knew that they loved him, and I knew that they were trying to help. He promised that he'd talk to them. I began to feel that the fight was to keep Bob and I united in our plan.

****

In the middle of all of this, the life insurance agent called again. He guessed that it had been long enough and asked how everything was going. I told him that Bob had been diagnosed with bone marrow cancer, and we were just back from the Mayo clinic. His reaction astounded me.

"Well, there's not an insurance company in the world that will write him a policy now."

I was so astounded by his lack of sensitivity that I did not even respond. I was in shock. He spoke again, "You know, Kim, I can still write a policy for you. Why don't you let me send you the application, and you can just complete it yourself? There's no need for you to come back to my office; I know how busy you are. Just fill it out and mail it back to me with a check."

Right! Like I was going to give this man anything! I told him not to call me again. He had the audacity to send the application to my house anyway. I threw it away. How persistent was this dance partner going to be? I had already refused his advances, but he was starting to feel a bit pushy. Why would anyone in his right mind try to sell life insurance to a person whose spouse had just been diagnosed with an incurable disease? It was most definitely an attack of the enemy. Again I heard it in my head, "They all think that Bob's dying."

Amid these emotional distractions, Bob and I were starting to move forward with treatment. We'd gone back to the hematologist from the cancer center who had sent us to Mayo and told him we were going to have the transplant. In the meantime, Bob would take the high-dose steroids. He agreed with our decision and referred us to a bone marrow specialist in Denver. It was still October, and we were already going to the BMT doctor. We were starting to fight the disease already, and on this front at least, things were right on track.

I thought that we were doing so well. I thought I was holding myself together. One little blip made me realize how tightly we were wound. On the way to the BMT doctor's office, I gave Bob the wrong directions. Blip. We got lost. He started yelling at me, and I yelled back. Both of us completely overreacted.

"I'm sorry. I guess I'm really more nervous than I realize," he said.

"Me, too," I replied. "Let's say a prayer before we go in, okay? We have to stay together through this; we can't take our anxiety out on each other."

We prayed that God would calm our fears and help us to have the strength to get through this visit.

Bob then asked God to let us know that we were doing the right thing, and then he said, "God, please let us know we're in the right place."

We walked into the offices. They were bigger and nicer than the cancer center that I had worked at in St. Louis, but not quite as overwhelming as the Mayo Clinic. I remember thinking, just the right size. Not too big, not too small. I read the doctor's names on the wall. Wow! There were a lot of them. We signed in and sat in the waiting room that consisted of nine chairs, a couch, and an aquarium. I watched the fish, remembering that I'd read somewhere that watching fish swim was supposed to be calming. I didn't feel calm. A woman came from the back and called Bob's name. We quietly walked back to a small area where she asked him to sit so she could take his vital signs. As she wrapped the blood pressure cuff around his upper arm, she asked, "How are you today?"

"Well, being that I'm here, not so good. I guess!" Bob attempted to joke.

What she said next was an answer to the prayer we had just prayed in the car. She bent over to remove the cuff, looked Bob square in the eyes, and said, "Then you're in the right place." Bob and I looked at each other and smiled. We were ushered into the exam room and waited for Dr. Jeffries. He came in, introduced himself, and told Bob, "You're about my age. What do you do for a living?"

They discussed our business, Bob's hobbies, and our life in general. It seemed like a social meeting just to get to know each other. We immediately liked him. Soon enough he talked about the disease, and he seemed impassioned by what he was saying. He showed us a slide show on his laptop; he'd just returned from a conference on myeloma. He told us that though the disease was a rare type, it was still considered a myeloma as far as treatment was concerned, so we would hear people calling it myeloma.

He told us, "You and I know it is Kappa Light Chain Deposition Disease, but when people talk about your myeloma, you don't have to correct them, just nod your head."

I didn't like it being called "his" myeloma, like he had ownership of it. I didn't like that at all. It was the enemy's myeloma, not Bob's. Somehow calling it his made it seem familiar, even friendly. We wouldn't accept that.

We heard again that the disease was incurable, but Dr. Jeffries agreed to do his best to take care of Bob and try to put this disease into remission. An autologous stem cell transplant, one in which Bob would donate and then receive his own stem cells back, was the treatment of choice. He told us the same thing that the bone marrow specialist at Mayo had, but this time we were listening better. We had had time for the information to sink in. He told us that we could possibly even do the transplant as an outpatient. Bob would be able to come home every night.

They would draw blood and then send us back to the hematologist until we were ready for transplant. Bob would stay on the steroids for a few months and see if his disease would go away. We needed his bone marrow to be "clean" before they harvested the stem cells to use them for the transplant. They would start talking with our insurance company and arrange pre-certification. We left, satisfied with everything we'd heard. We had a plan and were making progress. We knew it was going to be hard, but we were on the right path.

7
That's Gonna Leave a Mark

We went back to the hematologist for the next two months while Bob took high dose Decadron. Over the course of this treatment, Bob's weight varied from his normal one-hundred and sixty-five pounds up to one-hundred and ninety pounds. It was not uncommon for him to gain or lose fifteen pounds over the course of a weekend. It was the first time that the disease showed itself to us. One morning before work I was in the bathroom, and I heard Bob call from the bed, "Kim! Can you come here and look at something?"

I walked in to see the covers pulled back, and Bob's legs exposed. His ankles and feet were swollen. I assessed the level of edema, like a good nurse. I pushed my fingers into the swollen ankle flesh, and I counted as the indentations remained for a full two seconds. I stated out loud, "two plus pitting edema," walked back into the bathroom, and cried.

Why? I hated this disease. I hated that it was taking my husband. It seemed like it was winning. Two plus pitting ankle edema is not normal! The enemy had left a mark. It was still there, and it was showing itself to us, taunting us! I calmed myself the best I could, told Bob it would be okay and that he should just get ready for work. He was visibly scared. I was, too. I could hardly talk. I told him we needed to pray; we shouldn't be afraid. He agreed. We looked to each other for support, but neither of us had anything to give. We were scared together. How could swollen ankles scare us so much? We'd been to doctors who had told us that Bob had an incurable disease and walked out less scared than we were now! We were seeing the disease. We were finally seeing what it was doing to him, and we were petrified.

On the way to work, we stopped at Hope's house, a very dear friend. We'd met her approximately five years earlier at church. The relationship that we'd grown into having with her was not one of happenstance. It was truly a divinely planned meeting. I met her at a prayer meeting; I had never been to one before. Our church had small groups that met in different member's homes. These groups were designed for church members to get to know each other better, to study the Bible together, to help each other through life, and to learn to get closer to God together. The first meeting that I'd ever attended, I met Hope. I remember she opened the meeting with a prayer. As I listened to her pray, I thought, "Oh, my gosh! I want to learn to pray like that!" She spoke to God like nothing I'd ever heard before. She talked to him so sweetly, like she knew Him. She was so reverent yet so intimate. Just listening to her, I could tell that she had the type of relationship with God that I wanted.

After the meeting, she came to me and asked if I would go with her to pray for a friend of hers. I was taken back. I didn't even know this woman. Why would she ask me to go pray for someone with her? She told me that she knew that she was to ask me. I didn't ask her how she knew. I was just trying to figure how to get out of this praying-for-a-stranger thing. She was so bold in asking, so confident. I asked her what her friend needed prayer for, thinking this would give me more time to come up with an excuse. When she told me, I stopped trying to find a way out of it and immediately knew that I was to go. Her friend had breast cancer and was having a bone marrow transplant later that week. Hope wanted me to take her to the hospital and pray for her friend Sue before the transplant.

I heard myself speak, "I used to be an oncology nurse. I worked with transplant patients." I knew now that I was in, no turning back now. Hope smiled, a very knowing, sure-of-herself, but not conceited-looking smile.

When we arrived at the hospital, Hope told me that she wanted me to come into the BMT room and meet Sue. I remember thinking that I was somehow intruding in this woman's life. Would she ask me to leave? Would she want me to wait outside? Maybe I would tell Hope that I should wait in the hallway. I quickly learned that I wasn't just along for the ride. Hope wanted me to go into the room and pray for Sue with her, and she wouldn't take, "no" for an answer.

This was such a strange thing for me to do. I'd prayed for people before, even prayed for patients whom I'd cared for, but never had I driven a stranger to the hospital to pray for another stranger. This whole experience was strange for me. I didn't know why I was there, but I somehow knew that I must be obedient. That is exactly how I felt. Obedient. I remember telling Hope that was how I was feeling.

When we arrived in Sue's hospital room, she greeted us with a warm smile. She was thin and pale, with a floral print bandana wrapped around her head, a look that I was all too familiar with. She smiled the sweetest smile upon seeing Hope. They hugged, and Hope introduced me. "Sue, this is Kim. She's in our Bible Study, and she's here to pray for you with me. And you'll never believe it! She's an oncology nurse! Isn't God perfect?"

Sue held her frail hand out to me. As I took it in mine, I smiled at her and agreed immediately, God was perfect. The nurses walked in with the cooler containing Sue's stem cells. They set the cooler down and told us they'd be right back to begin. Hope went into action. She grabbed my hand and told me to come pray for the stem cells with her. We all placed our hands on the cooler and listened to Hope pray for God's touch, for purity, for health. We all prayed for God to be present and to give Sue the strength that she would need. The nurses came back. We stayed for the infusion and watched Sue receive "new life." I had watched stem cell transplants before, even preformed them myself. Never had I witnessed one from this angle. Never had I felt like one sent to pray. Hope and I left Sue. She had done well but was tired. I took Hope home and drove myself to work with such a strange feeling. I knew that I was meant to do what I had just done, but how did Hope know? She had seen something in me. Our relationship grew.

She became like a sister to me. Over the next five years, Hope would battle cancer herself. We watched her live those five years wholly by faith. She'd endured chemotherapy, radiation therapy, her husband leaving her, the loss of her job and finances. She'd trusted God for everything, and He'd provided. She was miraculously alive and well and there for us now.

Since Bob had been sick, Hope had been praying for us, a lot. The morning that we noticed the ankle swelling, we called her and asked if we could come to see her. We stopped in on our way to work. She was sitting on the floor in her living room, reading her bible. We sat on the floor with her. We told her about the swelling, how scary it was, and asked if she would pray for us. She did. She told us not to get scared about every new thing that we saw. She said to walk not by sight, but by faith. We knew that she knew what she was talking about. She was a great encouragement and support. We prayed and talked for a while until we felt better. Then she asked us each what we were afraid of most.

Bob said, "Dying." It hurt me to hear that he was afraid of death. It hurt to hear it stated out loud.

I said, "I know that faith can heal; I just don't know if Bob's faith is strong enough."

We cried and prayed some more. She prayed for Bob to get closer to God and for me to have peace.

8
What if We Lose?

Whether or not Bob had enough faith to be healed was a very common fear of mine. I knew that the Bible told me that faith could heal. I knew that Bob needed to just believe! I told him so. He didn't know. He was having a hard time with faith. He said, "I've asked God to help me to get closer to Him. I've prayed that I'd be able to know Him better, and this is what I get?! Cancer! I don't understand."

I didn't either, but I had a relationship with God, and I knew that He could take care of this. He was a good God, right? This would all work out: It just had to. Bob didn't know Him before all of this started; sure he went to church every Sunday, but he didn't really pray. He didn't talk to God like I did. He didn't *know* Him. That's what he'd asked for; a relationship with God. It's just that he'd have to go on this journey to find it.

Bob did say to me one day, "Maybe this is where I learn to pray. Maybe this is where I meet God."

Knowing that Bob was struggling to just get closer to God, I knew that asking him to just believe for a miracle healing would be a big stretch, so I asked God if my faith could do it. I asked if my faith could bridge the gap. I prayed that our marriage covenant would truly make us one flesh, and I begged God to see my faith as his…just until he found his own.

I prayed daily that God would give Bob the spirit of wisdom and revelation to know Him better, and I begged God to see him and me as one. Bone of his bone, flesh of his flesh. I dug through the Bible again and wondered where I could find an answer.

I found a story of a man who asked Jesus to heal his child. Jesus said He would because the man had such great faith. He didn't say the child had such great faith but that the father did. There was one story that helped. God had healed someone on someone else's faith. If God would do it for this man; He would surely do the same for me, wouldn't He? He would answer my prayer because of my faith. I also studied what God had to say about marriage. It was made to be a covenant relationship, a profound mystery. "For this reason a man will leave his father and mother and be united to his wife, and they will become one flesh." (Genesis 2:24, NIV Bible) Bob and I were one flesh. We were one. If we were one, then he could share in my faith. I would intercede for him. If this was a journey between Bob and God, between them would be me showing him the way, leading by my faith. I prayed for the strength to hold him up while he was weak, and I asked God to hold me.

These studies, these revelations that I had from this studying provided me with the strength I would need later. I truly would be not only Bob's faith, but also Bob's strength and Bob's voice.

I continued to pray for Bob. I continued to talk to him about his faith. I begged him to read his Bible. I just wanted to *know* that he had the faith to be healed. He tried; he truly did, yet to me it seemed that he cared more about what would happen at work, what would happen to him, his body, and how he could control it all. He wasn't honestly trusting God yet. I knew this wouldn't be easy for him, but I had faith that God would see us through.

One day early on in this journey, my brother Rusty called me. He lives in St. Louis, but we are very close. He introduced me to Bob; Bob and he are also very close. He called one day and said, "The weirdest thing happened to me today. I was driving down the road thinking about you and Bob and everything that you guys are going through, and God talked to me. Now don't think I'm crazy; I'm not hearing voices or anything, but I know it was God. He told me that I should tell you to get closer to Him."

I immediately started to cry. I had this feeling like everything around me had stopped; everything became silent except that statement: Get closer to Him. For a moment in time, there was nothing else but that: Get closer to Him. I thanked Rusty and told him that I didn't think he was crazy. I thought about what God was saying. Get closer. It scared me. What did that mean? I was going to need to get closer to God; I was going to need to be very close to Him. I was going to need to start hearing Him talk to me. God was already starting to speak.

There was another voice besides Rusty's that day. In the brief moment between his saying, "God said to get closer to Him" and my starting to cry, I heard something else. In my mind, in my spirit, I don't know. But I can hear it today as clearly as I heard it then.

"What if you lose it all?"

I ignored that question. Later that day, I heard it again. I was turning to throw a piece of paper into the trash can beside my desk, and I heard it again exactly as before, "What if you lose it all?" It caught my breath this time, and as I threw the paper into the trash can, I answered the question as if it were coming from God.

"I will still love you, God. I will still love you."

* * * * * * *

As Bob and I were getting ready for the transplant, we were also getting ready for the business changes. We had done as Paula knew we must: We hired an estimator. We'd never had a full-time estimator, besides Bob. It was a bit scary. I kept feeling like I was trying to replace Bob. I knew that it was a fear that was based on nothing but fear itself. Why would I think that Bob was leaving; he was only going to have a bone marrow transplant? We would find another estimator that Bob would "break-in" and help, then Bob would be down a few weeks. When Bob came back to work, he'd have an estimator who would help him. It would work out just fine; in the end, we'd even be better off. Bob wouldn't have so much pressure on him. He'd be able to share the burden of estimating with someone. It would work out just fine.

We started interviewing. Bob was still on the steroids and staring to look puffy. He was undergoing other changes as well. He was tired, emotional, and just not as "with it" as usual. I wasn't ignoring what was happening. I wasn't denying what was happening, but I couldn't just bow to it. I couldn't fall apart every time I saw something that reminded me that he was sick. I had to keep fighting. I fought every day. I'd hear his voice sounding weaker and fight the urge to cry. I'd see the swelling on his feet, his face, even his abdomen, and fight the fear. I'd watch him work less and less hours and fight the thoughts that I was not only losing my husband, but my business as well.

I fought. I would speak to the fear. "Fear, I resist you. I'm not afraid; God's on my side." I spoke that often.

As we interviewed, I kept thinking how sad it was that these people weren't meeting the real Bob. They were meeting this sick Bob, this imposter of my husband, imposter of a boss. As we interviewed, I realized that we'd need not someone whom Bob could train, but someone who would be able to be thrown right into the mix. He wouldn't be getting much training from this imposter Bob. I turned to my journal to unleash my thoughts.

> *God, I'm tired, but I can't be tired yet. Please give me strength. Work – we need help, Lord. We need help estimating and someone to be the "head." Jobs aren't going well. Hard to find work, then hard to make a profit. I begin to think we should scale back, slow down, lay off, cut the fat. Is this defeat? Is this wisdom? God, I need to hear from you. Bob isn't himself and won't be for awhile. He's not the same. I know he's sick, but he's different, too. Scared, weak, confused. Not Bob anymore. Can we, should we, slow down at work? Help me to find an estimator, God. Tell me where to go and what to do. This is Your business, God. I'm scared. Who is going to take care of me? Who is going to take care of this business, our employees? You will. I must have patience. God, You will take care of it all. Blessed. Blessed health, blessed family, blessed business. No fear. In speaking these things, I am not showing a lack of faith! I voice my concerns and fear like a confession before You. You hear me and heal me. This is my cry for help, God. Hear my spirit, not my flesh. Heal me, spirit and flesh. I will not falter, I will not grow faint. Faith. Word of God, speak. I am a warrior who is tired.*

9
Health Care Reform

As we tried to patch the ensuing holes in our company, our health insurance company was creating new holes in our lives. They assigned us a case manager to "help" with all of our insurance needs. In actuality this case manager was assigned to "help" the insurance company keep costs down.

Our first case manager was a woman named Cathy. Cathy was a registered nurse and led me to believe that she was very concerned with our well-being and smooth transition through this process. The first conversation that I had with Cathy was one in which she told me that she wasn't "very familiar with myeloma," but that she would read up on it and be more informed the next time we talked. Why hadn't she "read up on it" before we talked? She wasn't very professional. She said that she'd speak with the oncologist's office to find out what treatment plans were warranted and get back to me.

I already know treatment plans. Who did this stranger think she was? She "wasn't very familiar with myeloma," yet she would be the one to talk to our oncologist about treatment?! I don't think so. Bob and I had already gone down that road, remember? We were already busy trying to convince his family that we didn't need them to second guess every decision that we'd made, but at least they were concerned with Bob's well-being. This stranger was only concerned with economics. What would be cheapest? What would the insurance company say was the best? They didn't even know us! How could they tell us what was best? I was infuriated.

Finally, Cathy called and said she'd checked with our oncologist's office and had been convinced that a bone marrow transplant was warranted. She had given us permission to start looking for a hospital to have the transplant. I didn't thank her. She'd obviously brushed up on myeloma and its insurance-approved treatment options. I explained to her that we had already picked a hospital and a BMT specialist. She explained to me that we couldn't just pick a hospital. We would have to have the insurance company's permission, and even worse, we would need to pick a hospital and doctor that was on their approved list.

There was not a hospital or doctor in Colorado that was on their list; she would fax over the list of approved hospitals in other states. I began to cry. I didn't like that I was crying to a complete stranger. She had obviously had a few psychology classes in her training because she started her canned apology and sympathy. "I'm sorry that it has to be this way. I know how you must feel, but we only want what's best for him. I understand how hard this is for you."

"Really?" I said to her, "You do? Do you have a husband with an incurable disease? Did you just find out that he needs a transplant, and you'll have to move to another state for treatment?"

"No, but I can imagine. I've done this for a long time. We only approve the best hospitals, and the one in Colorado just lost our approval because the doctors have moved to another hospital. We haven't approved the new hospital yet." She had just shown her hand; it was about the money. They hadn't negotiated a price with the new hospital; therefore, it wasn't on the list of "best hospitals" yet.

"You can't imagine what we're going through; don't pretend you can. We can't go to another state. We have two daughters here; they need us. We have a business and employees here; they need us. There are people here who depend on us. We can't leave. We have to find a way to do this in Colorado."

"If this were my husband, I'd care more about his going to the best hospital and less about my job. You can get a new job."

I cussed at her. Wow, a new emotion. Anger. This one I liked. I told Cathy that I was getting ready to lose my *bleeping* temper, and I didn't want to do that on the phone with her listening.

She told me that I could say anything to her because that's what she was there for. I told her I wouldn't share any more feelings with her. I refused to vent to a complete stranger; I refused to let this woman who cared about nothing but what our crisis was costing her company to listen to me. I would not let her hear me fall apart. I told her not to call back, that I'd call her, and I hung up.

I later called my insurance company and told them to assign a new case manager. I was finished with Cathy; I was firing her. Maybe there was another case manager who had listened better in her psychology classes. I asked to speak to her supervisor and told her that Cathy obviously needed to work in a different area of the company. She didn't have the compassion for the job she had been assigned. Her supervisor agreed to take her off of our case. She reiterated what Cathy had said about finding a new center for transplant, but she was at least much more professional about it.

She concurred with my assessment that the insurance company was only waiting on the hospital and their board to come to an agreement on a contract price that was acceptable to both the hospital and the insurance company. The hospital and doctors that we had chosen would soon be an insurance-approved site, but the numbers had not been crunched yet. They were still in negotiation. Bob had unfortunately been diagnosed and needed treatment before negotiations were completed. I tried to explain to her that our going out of town and receiving a housing allowance would probably wind up costing the insurance company more in the long run.

She said, "Maybe so, but this is how it works." Boy, was the insurance company messed up! They were trying to do what was cheapest and were actually ready to pay more. This was not a battle that I could fight right now, though. I couldn't take on the entire insurance industry, I had another battle that had already started.

10
Have No Doubt

Everything was starting to fall apart again. What the heck was going on? Bob and I had made our decision, and we had asked God to give us a sign. He had. We were "in the right place," remember? Were we so unbelievably inept that we couldn't make this decision on our own? Why were so many people trying to control what was happening? God, we just want to be where You want us; where do You want us? Speak to us, again.

November 14, 2003:

The hospital will not be a "designated provider of bone marrow transplants" until negotiations are complete. God, what is happening? I still love You, God, but I'm so confused. Are You allowing this to happen? Is everything being taken away – my husband, my family, my business? Are we being tested? What really matters? God. God will never go away. Why do I feel so defeated right now? Bob is so sick, and I'm so bad at taking care of him. I just want him to get up and stop being sick, to be Bob!! Irrational thought. This is just the beginning. Where will we go, God? Will we have to move? Can we stay here? Can I be certain that we will stay here? Can I have faith that we will stay here, God? I know You know what's best; You are in control. Tell me, God, if I should walk here or there. Speak this way or that. Tell me, God. I don't know where to go without Your lead. Lead me. Only by Your word, God, only by Your word. This is not my battle, not

my fight. Make a way, Lord. I need help with work, too, not just for me and my family but for others.
Isaiah 40:31 Those who hope in the Lord will renew their strength.
Isaiah 41:13 For I am the Lord, your God, who takes hold of your right hand and says to you, Do not fear; I will help you. (NIV Bible)

We had talked to so many doctors, had been to the Mayo Clinic, had consulted with my past colleagues, and we were convinced we were doing the right thing and that we were in the right place. Above all else, we felt at peace with our decision. Why were we being made to doubt this decision again?

* * * * * * *

A BMT Nurse Coordinator whom I had worked with in St. Louis and whom I respected greatly said to me one day, "Kim, can I give you some advice?"

"Sure!"

"You and Bob need to make your decision and stick with it. Don't doubt yourselves. It's important to go forward after you've made the decision."

Unfortunately, Bob's family agreed with the insurance company and wanted us to seek other doctor's opinions. "What would it hurt?" was a question that his family asked often. Though I felt that it was somewhat of a rhetorical question, I had an answer. It was an answer that I knew, that I lived, but that I wouldn't verbalize until much later. What would it hurt to continue to look for answers in man? In a drug? In a new hospital or treatment modality?

It would hurt our faith, our peace, our belief. It would hurt our moving forward. It would impede our progress. It would confuse us; it would throw doubt and fear back into the mix. Bob and I had now been through approximately five months of doctors' visits, lab tests, x-rays, ultrasounds, biopsies, and education concerning this disease. I had been an oncology nurse for eight years, a good one, too. We had spoken with enough doctors, had seen enough results, had discussed enough options. We knew what we wanted to do. We knew where we wanted to do it, and we knew that we had picked the right hospital and doctor. We had made lists of what was important in the decision-making process. There were also social and psychological issues to take into consideration.

Bob and I would be better able to cope at home, in a familiar place with our family. Aimie and Katie needed us near, and we needed to be in our own house, be near work, our church, and my parents. We'd made our decision. We'd told everyone that we'd made our decision. We were finished with this part of the battle. We didn't ask for them to second guess us; we asked for their support. Now all hell was coming against us. Why were we being made to doubt our decision? What would it hurt? Plenty.

Doubt, fear, worry: All are weapons of the enemy. My weapon was faith. Believe. Believe that we are in the right place, doing the right thing. Doubt was a wicked tool of the enemy.

I asked Bob if I could speak with his family and tell them not to fear. I asked if we could sit down with them and explain what was happening the way that I was seeing it: as an attack from the enemy. Bob said no. He didn't think that they would understand; he wasn't sure that he understood it completely.

I wanted to talk to his family, but I obeyed Bob's request.

****

There are many jokes made about in-laws, about many psychologists making a good living based on therapy related to in-laws. Why? Because families are different. Bob was always trying to adjust to my family, and I was always trying to adjust to his. Normal in-law stuff, normal things to do when you get married. However, in the middle of Bob and me trying to adjust to each other's families, we were also trying to adjust to this non-normal event happening in our lives. We were not so sensitive to our in-law relationships at this time. We were trying to adjust to this battle with death. We were becoming less and less tolerant of anything that was not normal. Sometimes that intolerance became evident in our relationships with our families.

Our families called often. They wanted to know how they could help; there were all feeling helpless and wanted something to do. We gave the same answer that we gave everyone: Just be there for us and support us. We all decided that it would be best for Bob's parents to move to Denver for six months in order to be close by for the transplant and recovery.

Upon his parents' arrival, we received a barrage of phone calls. Each of his brothers and sisters called, "What do you want Mom and Dad to do? They want to help. Just tell them."

I answered, "I don't know. We'll ask if we need anything. It's just nice that they're here." They didn't accept that very well.

Bob told them when they called, "I don't really need anything right now. I'll let you know."

Have I made it clear that it was hard for Bob and me to accept help? We had never had to rely on anyone before. We were trying to work, hire people, and convince our employees that we would make it through this. Every time someone tried to convince us that we needed their help, it was as if they were telling us we were failing. It was such a struggle to accept the help with gratitude.

We felt like we didn't need anyone. Why was everyone there trying to convince us that we did? There was too much planning, too much of everyone planning our lives out for us. I felt like we were in a cage, and everyone was standing around looking in at us and deciding what was best for us, what was best for our lives.

11
Fearful Anger

I was so angry. I remembered in school learning the five states of grieving: Denial, Anger, Bargaining, Depression, Acceptance. I had gone through each one of them, sometimes all in one day. Anger was my favorite. It somehow gave me an outlet for all of my emotions. I was mad as I could be, at anyone and everyone. I would see people in the grocery store whom I didn't know and be mad at them because they looked happy. I had friends who were planning a vacation, and I was so mad that they were going on with their normal, happy lives. How dare they vacation while we were enduring this fight for our lives? What kind of friends were they? I was especially mad at anyone who wanted to help us. They were constant reminders to us that we were sick.

I was even, at times, mad at Bob. How could he do this to me? How could he get sick? He was supposed to take care of me! He was my husband! How was I going to do all of this without him?

The only person that I wasn't mad at was God. I was too afraid to get mad at Him. I'd been mad at God before in my life, and it didn't get me anywhere. I respected and revered Him. I knew He had a plan; I didn't understand it, but I knew that He was in control. I couldn't get mad at Him; He was the only one who could truly help. I continued to trust Him. I continued to pour myself out to Him. He was the only one to Whom I could really open up. I shared my fear, my sorrow, and my anger with Him. I begged Him to help.

December 1, 2003:

Be the lifter of my head, God. Help me, deliver me. Deliver me from myself, from my thoughts, from my fears. I don't care how the circumstances look; help me see past this mountain. I believe You can do it, God. Help me. Please shadow Bob in the healing of Your wings. I'm scared to death, God. Things seem to just be happening around me. Life is changing so quickly; everything is different. Everything is scary. We have no control. Everything is just happening. I feel so helpless, God. Bob has to get closer to You. He has to if he's to live. I feel that the very reason that I fell in love with this man is his downfall right now. He is so self-sufficient, so in charge. He does it all. He's "the guy." Well, now the guy needs help, and he's a little lost at how to get it. He doesn't know how to ask for help. He never had to. He's never needed anyone. Just himself. Now he needs You, God. He needs to ask You for help. He doesn't know how. Help us, God. We need help, and we don't know how to receive it.

Psalm 68:35: God gives power and strength to his people. (NIV Bible)

On the outside, Bob and I were trying to maintain a sense of control, a sense of peace. Inside, we were a mess. We were scared that the insurance company would win, and we would have to move. We took the advice of a few doctors and past colleagues of mine and spoke to our attorney.

We had a corporate attorney, but he only dealt with our business and contract issues. I thought that he could at least point me in the right direction. When I explained what was happening, he told me that his wife had undergone a bone marrow transplant, and he knew exactly what we were going through. Thank you, God! He said he would make a few phone calls and see what he could do. I felt better.

At the same time, the insurance company was faxing us a list of the hospitals and doctors that we were to choose from located in Nebraska, St. Louis, and Arkansas. The crazy thing is that they were sending us housing allowance forms, meal allowance forms, all of which they were prepared to pay for in another state. According to them, we needed to go see one of these doctors for a second opinion, our seventh "second" opinion. They were prepared to pay for the trip. We called our Denver doctor and asked if he would give us an opinion on who we should see; we were going to humor the insurance company.

He wouldn't give us a name for a second opinion. "No. I'm so convinced that we'll have the designated facility authorization from your insurance company that I refuse to give you the name of another doctor. The negotiations are going very well. You will be ready for transplant by January. Have you spoken to an attorney yet? The insurance company can make a special allowance for you before negotiations are complete; they need to be forced sometimes."

It was all getting so confusing. I disliked lawyers, not individually, but generally. I disliked having to use one to get what I felt we were entitled to anyway. We paid our insurance premiums, and we played by their rules. Why were we having to fight to get what we'd paid for? We were saving them money, for goodness sake! I also felt like in speaking to any attorney, we were not trusting God. It was a confusing thing for me.

I was at my parents' house one day, and I started venting about the insurance company and lawyers and the whole thing. I tried not to let go like this very often to anyone but God, but this was my family. We'd always shared everything. We were very open and honest. It wasn't always easy, but it was always true. I had been having trouble sharing my feelings during the beginning of this event in our lives. I didn't know how to share. I was afraid to open up. In the beginning, it was because I was still trying to deny that Bob had cancer. I didn't want to open up and vent now because I didn't want to be weak. I wanted to be confident, have faith, and know that he'd survive this. If I talked too much about it, I'd break down. I saved that for when I was alone with God.

This day, as I was venting, I was starting to lose control a bit, and I took some of my anger out on my mom. I was mad that everyone was trying to help; I felt that everyone was trying to take control of our lives.

I cried and said, "I don't want everyone to help us! Why can't we just be left alone? Why do we need help?" She listened as I went on, "Everyone! My family, his family, friends, people from church, Aimie and Katie's friends' parents, neighbors, work colleagues, everyone wants to know what they can do! I don't have time to make lists for everyone. What do they want from me?"

"They just care, Kim." Now she was trying to help.

"When we need something, we'll ask! Why are they pressuring us to tell them what to do!? This isn't about everyone else; it's about us!" I yelled.

"Everyone is suffering, Kim, not just you and Bob. We all just want to help." I hated that answer.

"Let's talk about everyone else. How is it affecting their lives? Do they live with Bob? Do they sleep with him every night? Do they watch his body change as I have? Have they lost their husband? Have they lost their business partner? No. Big deal, their lives aren't changing as mine is!" I was mad at everyone who was not losing what I was losing.

"I don't know what we want. I don't know what we need. We want our normal life back. We want cancer gone! Can anyone do that?! That's what we need. We need this to go away. Who can do that?!" I was yelling at her as if it were all her fault. Anger, albeit misdirected, sure felt good. "And what if we have to go to another state? Who will help then? We'll be alone, like at Mayo. I'll go nuts away from home! I can't do this somewhere else! I won't!"

My mom jumped in to try and help answer my questions. She had listened but hadn't truly heard what I was saying this time. I wasn't asking her to fix this; I was merely venting.

She began, "You know if they make you go somewhere else, I'm sure there will be housing near, and we can all take turns staying with you. We'll work it out." A very motherly, supportive thing to say, right? Wrong. I replied out of fear, confusion, but mostly anger. I was mad that the insurance company was trying to tell us what to do, trying to run our lives, and it seemed like his family was agreeing with the insurance company, and now my mom was bending to them, too. To me it was like picking sides. Are you for us or against us? The insurance company was definitely against us, and now my mom seemed to be on their side! How could she be siding with the enemy?

"Why are you saying this?!" I cried. "We're not staying in 'housing' somewhere! We're staying home! I don't give a crap what the insurance says; we're not leaving!"

She was hurt; I could tell by her body language. "I'm sorry….I was just saying…"

I didn't let her finish, I cut her off in my still-fuming-anger, "You were just saying 'Give In'! Do what the insurance company says! Let them decide, let them win. Let them take us away from our support system." I got up and walked toward the door. "Well, we won't. Thanks for dinner." I slammed the door as I left.

****

It was so clear to me; we were in a battle. Every detail mattered, every detail was either going to aid us or our enemy. Being away from home, fighting on foreign soil would aid our enemy. That was no good. I needed to fight from my own home, with my own support system, at my own church. I would not leave Aimie and Katie, and I would not leave my home. Why were so many people trying to get us to leave home? Why were so many people siding with the enemy?

My mom was only trying to help. I could see that, but I couldn't explain to her that she wasn't really helping. For heaven's sake, how could I tell her, or anyone for that matter, what I was thinking? They'd think I'd lost my mind.

Early December, 2003:

Grieving, are we all grieving? No, do not be defeated. God, help me out of this. Deliver me from my thoughts, from myself. I don't care how my circumstances look. Help me to see past this mountain. So the insurance company says that we have to move. Is it worth fighting? Whatever will be, will be. God, You are in control. I am catatonic. My old self would be writing letters, making calls, not letting them get away with this. Where is that old self? I'm either too stressed to act or too scared into this catatonic state of doing nothing. God, can I do nothing, but pray, and wait upon You? Move, God. Remember when we were at the cancer center, and the woman said, "You're in the right place'? Remember that gut feeling that Bob and I had? Were we wrong? God, I don't want to go away. I don't want to live somewhere else. But if it is Your will—Your way—then so be it! I know that You are involved. I know that You see the beginning and the end. You know where we belong; You know where we should go. Take us wherever You want or need us to be. Protect us, God. Be with us. I'd rather be with You in a strange place than at home without You. Please hear my heart. Hear my cry. I love you, God. I want what you will. Help me to plant that deep inside; let me feel it everyday growing in me. Faith.

Bob's family tried to help, too, and Bob had just as much difficulty trying to convince them that he didn't need help. Bob didn't yell at his parents the way that I yelled at mine. He felt bad, guilty that he was sick. He knew that they were frightened, and he was upset that they were suffering because of him. He tried mostly to console them.

I asked him to tell them not to be afraid in front of him. I asked him to explain how frightened he was and to tell them that their fear only made it worse on him. I told him to please tell them to support us and join us in this fight.

He told me, "It's okay, I can handle whatever they say to me. They're just scared. They are trying to help me; this is what they do. They are trying to take care of me, and this is how they make decisions. They have to explore every option to try and make the best decision they can. I can take what they have to say; I won't let it bother me. I know it's my own decision, Kim, but they have to feel like they have some control."

I thought it was a bad battle plan to fight on two fronts at the same time. I tried to explain to him that it seemed to me like all of this investigating other options was opening the door to doubt and fear. He didn't understand what I was saying; I don't even know if I totally understood.

They invited him to dinner one night in their newly-leased apartment. They were going to have dinner with the boys. My fear was that when they had him alone, they would fill him up with the doubt, fear, worry, the sheer panic that they were reveling in. I didn't want him to go alone. He promised me that he'd be okay. I knew that if I were near, they wouldn't speak to him in the same way. I was convinced that my faith was protecting us. The enemy saw my faith and also saw Bob's lack of faith. If he could separate Bob and me, he could divide and conquer. I'd read in the Bible that I was to know my enemy's tactics. I underestimated him. What better tools for the enemy than Bob's own family? They loved him, and he loved them. Even though it was unintentional, could they be trying to hurt him? Bob wasn't using the same filter that I was. I honestly began to listen and see everything through the "Does this come from God or the enemy?" filter. Doubt, fear, worry, anxiety: These were all weapons of the enemy. I would not stand for them in myself, so how could I put up with them in others?

The night Bob went to have dinner with his parents and brothers without me, I went out to dinner with Stan and his girlfriend. Bob called me at approximately 9:00 P.M.

"When are you coming home?" He sounded like he was crying. Bob rarely cries.

"I can come home whenever you want me to."

"Now."

I left in a hurry. What was wrong now? Was it more swelling, another symptom to deal with, had he just realized what was happening? It was okay, we'd pray, ask God for strength. He just needed to boost his faith up a notch. It was just a step backwards, but we'd get through it. When I got home, he was already in bed and crying.

"What's wrong?" I hugged him.

"My parents and brothers think I should see another doctor. They don't know if we're doing the right thing. I feel like they ambushed me. They're so scared; they don't think we've given this enough thought. They think maybe we should get a second opinion. Are we doing the right thing? Do we know what we're doing?" He was truly in a panic. I hadn't seen him like this ever before.

I reacted in anger, again to the enemy, not to Bob. "Second opinion?! Where have they been? We've already had six doctors tell us that transplant is the treatment of choice. We've been to the freaking Mayo clinic. We've spoken with the doctor who wrote the book that other doctors read on myeloma!"

He came back with what he'd been filled with all evening: "What would it hurt to see one more doctor? My brother has called a doctor in California. He talked to him for a long time. He says he's very nice and that he'd be happy to give us another opinion. They all think that I should see him. What do you think? I mean…what would it hurt?" He sounded completely lost. He sounded like a frightened little child, and I hated hearing him so scared.

"What would it hurt!? I don't know, Bob, you tell me! What is it hurting right now?" I paused and tried to bring my voice down a few decibels. "How do you feel about going to California to see another doctor, Bob? I'm confused as to why we've been fighting so hard to stay home if you want more opinions? How do you feel about leaving our home again? How do you feel right now, right this very minute?" Why was this so confusing?

"Confused, scared, I don't know," he began to cry again.

I waited for him to talk. Anger was in me and ready to jump out and yell at him. I wanted to scream, I wanted to tell him that if he and his family were going to plan this whole treatment course themselves without my involvement, then he could pack his bags and go move in with them. Why were they excluding me? Why was Bob planning this battle without me? We had included both of our families in on our plan, we had shared what we'd been through, and we had asked them for support. Why was he discussing treatment options and courses of action without me? Why did his family want to do this behind my back? Did they think I wanted to hurt him? Didn't they think I wanted what was best for us? I wanted to shake Bob. I wanted to cry, yell, and scream, "This is our life!" I didn't. I remained silent.

I know now that they only needed to speak with him alone because they were scared, and they didn't feel comfortable opening up in front of me. I also know the tactics of the enemy. Satan used their fear against us, if only they would have known. I wasn't prepared to give up my "control" of the situation. I couldn't. I was one with Bob. This is what I kept holding on to. Our oneness would allow

God to see him through my faith. I couldn't be angry now; I had to fight the anger. I had to unite with Bob.

Bob finally said, "Kim, I'm so confident, so at peace, and ready to face this transplant until I go see my family. I know we're in the right place. Remember that day we prayed and asked God to let us know, and He did? That was so cool. I really felt good about our decision. As soon as I talk with my family, I'm confused again. I get so scared. What if they're right? What if we need to keep looking?"

It was so clear to me, why couldn't he see? It was the enemy confusing them, confusing him. "Bob, can I tell you something? I want to explain how I feel and if after I explain this to you, you want to see ten more doctors, I'll go. Okay?"

"I'm listening." He sat up in bed.

I explained to him that I believed the Bible to be the true word of God. I told him that I believed that God was with us, and for whatever reason, this was the path laid before us. I was sure that we would walk it with God. However, as sure as I was that there was a God, I was just as sure that there was an enemy: Satan. I believed that Satan would do anything to steal, kill, and destroy our lives because the Bible said that's what he wanted to do. I told him I believed that now, more than ever, we must see everything as white or black: God or Satan. I told him that the Bible told us that we would fight spiritual battles and that this was a spiritual battle. I was believing and trusting God to help us, and I knew that Satan would do whatever he could to stop us from believing. He would use any means to get to us, even our families. I encouraged him to stand firm, believe the Bible, and resist the enemy and anything that comes from him. Doubt, fear, and worry were not from God. God's word told us to worry about nothing, pray about everything. God did not give us a spirit of fear. Trust God! It sounded so simple when said out loud. How could something so simple be so difficult?

I finished with telling him, "If you want to see more doctors, we will, but not because you're afraid or confused. We will not act on fear! We cannot let Satan direct our steps. Pick a number of consults that you feel comfortable with. How many doctors do you want to see before you're ready to decide? I will go with you to however many you want, but we must decide."

Bob calmed down, "We've had six doctors tell us the same thing. I don't need to hear it again. I don't want to leave the kids, leave home, and leave work. I know what I want to do. I'm doing it. We're in the right place. I'm sorry I freaked out. I don't want to worry anymore. I want to trust God the way you do, Kim. It's harder for me than for you, though. I don't get the same thing out of praying as you do. I'm trying. I've been asking God for a long time to help me get closer to Him, and this is what I get: cancer. It's not fair."

True, it wasn't, but the journey had begun. We just needed to keep walking through it. "I know, Bob, it's not fair. I don't understand why this is happening, either, we can't figure everything out, but we have to trust Him. We have nothing else. He knows best; I know it. We'll make it through this if we stay together: you, me, and God. We have to be one. I'll support whatever decision you make as long as we keep God involved."

Bob decided that he didn't need another consult, he was ready to trust God, and he was going to try harder to have faith in God and not in man. He knew God was there. He knew God would help, but he remained worried for his family.

"How can I tell them to stop worrying and stop looking for more doctors? They're so scared."

I told him that if they saw faith increase in him, maybe it would calm them. If they could see Bob's faith grow, their faith might grow. Maybe this was part of the reason for all of this, to share our strong faith with his family, so that they would come to know God in a more intimate way. He agreed that this would be a good thing for them. Unfortunately, they wouldn't be able to see Bob's faith grow; none of us would. It was done in secret, in a place where only Bob and God were let in.

That night, Bob took another over-the-counter sleep aid. I vowed it would be the last time that I would let the enemy scare my husband into tears. I would protect him from the enemy's schemes, no matter what that meant. I told Bob, "I will protect you from whatever the enemy throws at you, even if it involves your family. If you can't tell them that their worry and doubt is hurting you, I will."

He agreed to talk to them, but I don't believe he ever had the chance.

* * * * * * *

As I write these things, I realize how easy it is to attach the enemy status to anyone who did not stand on the rock of faith that I was standing on. I also realize this is not how God would have wanted it; I see now that I was afraid and I was bowing to fear. I bowed to fear of telling Bob's family about my faith. I was afraid to tell them of the faith that I was made of. I was afraid that they would think me nuts! I was afraid that if I told them that the enemy was trying to steal my faith by throwing doubt and fear at me, they would tell Bob that I had lost my mind. So instead, I just acted on my faith and didn't share it with them. I am sorry that I didn't share my faith and my belief with them. I am so sorry that I allowed them to travel this journey in fear, when I could have reached my hand out and offered them the same gift of faith that I had been blessed with. My fear of what they would think of me forced me to let them stay in their own fear. The enemy is very crafty. There was enough fear to go around, and he used it on all of us.

12
Distraction in the Basement

In the midst of these small battles, these family tug-of-wars that we were experiencing, we were still preparing for the true battle. All of the family concerns and all of the insurance problems were distractions from what we really should have been concentrating on. I knew what was coming, so I thought. The transplant would be one of the hardest things that Bob would ever go through. I prayed for strength. Things were changing so quickly. We'd hired more people at work to help us through the rough times that were to come. Bob and I were so preoccupied with the sickness, with that front of the battle, we lacked at work. I didn't care. If God wanted us to keep this business, we would. If not, I didn't care.

I honestly could not concentrate at work. How could I care about something so trivial when I was facing death every day? I prayed for our business, and I prayed that God would protect our workers and our jobs. That is all I had to give, prayer. I prayed for Paula, that she'd have the strength and ability to hold it all together. I prayed for my dad, who at that point was working everyday in our shop "helping out." He did more than help out; he practically ran things. I prayed for John, who had stepped up and stepped into a role of leadership to fill the gap that Bob's absence had left. I prayed for all of our employees.

We had a crew of approximately twenty men. Over the next year, we would lose over half of them. Paula said it was like separating the wheat from the chaff. The ones who fell by the wayside left for various reasons. The truth was that they all somehow saw the ship sinking. They were rats jumping overboard. As I was watching what was happening, I often wondered if God was taking it all away from us. Maybe we would lose it all. I didn't care; all I wanted was my husband. Work was a battle that I couldn't fight. I had to trust God that the people in charge would hold it all together until Bob and I came back.

* * * * * * *

Our new case manager from the insurance company kept in contact with me. She kept asking us to pick where we would go for treatment; we kept putting her off. We weren't able to put them off for too long because the side effects from the Decadron were worsening. Bob's body was changing so rapidly. He'd developed a rash from the steroids. His testicles swelled so that he could hardly wear pants, and he was forced to wear oversized sandals now because his feet wouldn't even fit into the three-sizes-too-large boots that we'd purchased.

He was becoming so compromised by the changes in his body that he wanted to stop the steroids. The doctors were satisfied with the fact that the disease seemed to respond to the steroids, but they agreed that Bob wouldn't be able to take this treatment too much longer. They, as we, were waiting for the insurance company to give us the green light for transplant. Bob and I felt as if we were in purgatory. It seemed so unfair that our lives were on hold while a group of men in starched shirts and business suits sat somewhere around a conference table negotiating how much money a bone marrow transplant was worth. In essence, they were negotiating how much Bob's life was worth.

We tried to work as much as we could, which for Bob was less than part-time. We spent most evenings at home with Katie, eating dinner, watching T.V., or hanging out with my family or his. We tried to relax; we tried to enjoy each other's company. I think we even learned to accept help.

So many friends of ours would call and say, "Don't cook tomorrow; we're bringing you dinner." They'd stop by, ring the doorbell, hand us the food, give us a hug, and leave. "If you need anything else, call." So many people sent cards and letters with prayers of support. Our families were there for us, to give us whatever we needed. We were truly blessed.

The doctors' visits continued, and the hematologist and nephrologist were concerned that Bob's kidneys were failing. They were afraid that his kidneys wouldn't be strong enough to make it through the transplant if the transplant weren't performed quickly enough. They put him on a reduced-sodium diet and low-protein diet. Most people who cooked for us prepared food as usual, so Katie and I would enjoy these meals prepared by friends and family while Bob followed a more strict diet. I am so thankful that friends and family continued to prepare food for Katie and me. Bob's appetite had changed drastically, and he was never really satisfied with anything anyway. He began to drink Boost and Ensure meal replacement drinks. He said, "Food isn't good anymore."

****

I don't know the reason why, if Bob were looking for something to take his mind off of the illness, or if he had finally completely lost his mind, but in the midst of this horrific time in our lives, he said to me one day, "Kim, I think we should finish our basement." I actually laughed out loud, thinking it was a joke.

We had talked of refinishing the basement before Bob got sick but had decided to put in on the back burner when he became sick. We agreed to keep the door shut and keep Bob upstairs. There would be no reason for him to visit the basement during his transplant, and we didn't need the additional stress.

So the day when Bob told me that he wanted to finish the basement, I didn't actually believe him. I knew Bob was in no physical shape to finish a basement. "Bob, why are you saying this? You know how stressful a remodeling project is. We've got so much going on in our lives."

"I know, Kim, but I think it would be good to do before my transplant. It'll keep me busy. And it needs to be cleaned up before the transplant."

Keep him busy?! What was he talking about? "No. We've already discussed this, and we've already decided we're not finishing our basement in the middle of this." I thought I had put my foot down. "There is no need for you to go into the basement while you are having your transplant. It's not dirty; it's just unfinished."

"We can do it. My parents will help." He was serious.

"So, let me get this straight," I started, "You want to remodel a basement right now while you are on high-dose steroids, your body is swelling so badly that you can't bend at the knees, you sleep about twelve hours per day, you can't even work a twenty-hour work week, we're going through our savings account on doctors' bills, and we're trying to mentally prepare for a bone marrow transplant. Do you think this is a good idea?"

He wasn't taking, "No," for an answer. He told me he was going to finish it with or without my help. I threw such a fit! I stomped out of the room crying, ran upstairs and threw myself across our bed, and screamed into my pillow until my head throbbed. Bob came into our bedroom and yelled over my screaming, "I have to do this! What will it hurt?"

There it was: What will it hurt? Try as I might, I couldn't convince him that it would hurt. I told him that he was too physically weak to do the job, while he argued that he could handle it. I told him that we didn't have the money to buy carpet, while he argued that it was a basement, and we could get the cheapest carpet we could buy. I told him that I wanted to spend time with him before the transplant and not be stressed out, while he said that I could spend time with him working on the basement. I told him that we didn't have time to do it, while he told me that we would have plenty of help from all of the family members who were looking for something to do to help us anyway. I cautiously questioned him, "Are we doing this to fulfill everyone else's need to feel helpful, Bob?"

He assured me that whether or not anyone helped, he was going to remodel the basement. I was beaten. As strongly as I felt that this was one of the craziest, stupidest, most irresponsible decisions that he had ever made, I could not convince my sickened and weakened husband not to do it. He won, so I jumped in with both feet and added a remodeling project to our already full plate of responsibilities. I tried to find as much help as possible to keep Bob from doing any of the physically taxing work.

The best way for me to describe the agony that this caused is by giving a few very specific examples of the labor involved. Bob would not allow anyone to physically exert themselves without helping, so he spent the next few weeks in our basement, and we lost Bob at work again.

Bob carried two fifty-pound buckets of drywall mud to the basement and suffered an inguinal hernia from the exertion, a hernia that he suffered from for over a year. His muscles had atrophied so badly from the disease process and the high-dose steroids that the exertion of lifting caused the hernia. The surgeon stated that although it was one of the largest hernias that he had ever seen, he didn't feel comfortable operating on Bob until the transplant was over, and Bob was on his way to healing again. Bob would have to live with the hernia for a year. Every time he complained about it, I smartly responded, "But just look at that basement!"

Bob decided to completely tear out the basement bathroom, drywall walls, shower and all. When the shower stall was removed, he found mold and cleaned up the mess himself. If he were concerned over the basement being messy, why was he stirring up this mess while being in a weakened immune state? The steroids had weakened his immune system so, that to this day I wonder if the demolition of that moldy bathroom didn't some how play into an infection that almost took his life. "But just look at that basement!"

Our remodeling stress was intensified by an accelerated schedule, lack of funds, a house full of unwanted opinions on decorating ideas, and the ever-present reminder of Bob's illness. The old Bob would have finished the space in his own way, on his own time, and with me at his side praising how talented he was. We had made such a good team in our past remodeling endeavors. We worked together, sweated together, created together. It was something that we "did" together.

Not this time. This time I hated the fact that I was picking paint and carpet while my mind was so preoccupied.

The only redeeming factor was that we finished so quickly and the hell that we endured was short-lived. While everyone else's desire to be helpful was met, Bob and I were pulling apart. At this time in our lives, we should have had evenings lying together on the couch, watching old movies, kissing and hugging. All I wanted was time alone with my husband. All I got was a husband who was wearing himself out, physically hurting himself, and frustrating himself with the realization that he couldn't do what he used to. I was so angry.

I took my anger out on Bob. When I'd see him sitting on the floor replacing an electrical outlet, I'd snap at him, "Why didn't you ask me to help?! Why are you doing this? Let it go!"

He wouldn't. He was driven to finish. Finish we did: new carpet, new paint, new bathroom. To this day I can't walk into our basement without thinking of the things that I would have done differently if we had remodeled under normal circumstances.

The basement taught me a lesson, though. It taught me that I wouldn't bend again to the pressures of someone else's need to feel helpful. This was about Bob and no one else. I again took on the role of being his protector. I was going to step in and be the strong one for a while. As much as I didn't want to be the strong one, I would. I had to. If being strong meant hurting people's feelings, so be it. I didn't have the energy to play games. I didn't have the hypocrisy to feel sorry for anyone else. I didn't feel that it was my place to take care of anyone else.

It's a very selfish thing. I became so intent on taking care of Bob and me that I even neglected our girls. Aimie was away at school and living her new life. She knew that Bob was sick, knew that it was serious, but she was engrossed in her new life as she should have been. Katie was lonely. She's a very quiet, introverted young lady, so it's hard to tell when she's really hurting. It takes effort to notice when she's hurt. I didn't put forth the effort; I just couldn't. She was going to school and doing well, was hanging out with friends, attending homecoming events, being a normal teenager.

One evening I told her that if she needed to talk to anyone, she could talk to me. I apologized for being so distant, so preoccupied, but assured her that I was concerned with her and how she was coping. She matter-of-factly told me that if she needed anything, she'd ask. I encouraged her to also talk with Grandma, Aunt Paula, or Aimie. I reminded her that they all were her support system as well. She knew. No big mushy conversation, just the facts. That was Katie. That is what I expected, and that is what I got.

13
God's Timing

It amazes me how awesome God's timing really is. We wonder why some things seem to take so long. If we would have had the transplant immediately, I would have never experienced the preparation that God had for me. The first week of December, while we were fighting the insurance company to give us permission to start a transplant, God was preparing a life-changing event for me.

Hope called me at work one morning, "Can you leave work?" There was an urgency in her voice that scared me.

"What's going on?" I asked, hoping that I wouldn't have to leave. There were so many things to take care of, so many days that I'd missed with doctors' visits. I felt almost guilty for missing so many days of work.

"Sue's husband called me; he wants me to go to the hospital and pray with her. She's been admitted to a hospice program, and they don't know how much longer she'll last, and she wants someone praying with her."

This is the same Sue that five years earlier Hope and I had prayed for during her bone marrow transplant. This is the same Sue that I met through Hope and the same Sue who had fought cancer for the past five years. Now she was dying. And Hope was asking me to go and pray? How dare her! Didn't she know what I was going through? Didn't she realize what this would do to me? I couldn't believe what she was asking of me.

"Hope, I can't. I just can't. This is too hard for me," I sounded so scared even to myself.

"Kim, you have to take me. You have to. Please, I don't have anyone else to take me, and I need a ride. We don't have a lot of time to waste," she was practically begging me.

"Can I just take you there and drop you off? What if I can't go in?" I was being talked into it.

I stood up and told Paula, "I can't believe her. How can she expect me to do this? Doesn't she understand what she's asking me?" I started to actually panic.

Paula, trying to help me, told me that I didn't have to go. "Don't go. Tell her that you can't."

I wanted to listen to Paula, I wanted to say, "No." I knew I couldn't. I didn't know why at the time, but I was being drawn to go. God had so much to give me out of the experience that I was walking in to. I cried as I drove to Hope's house. I walked into her living room, sat on her couch and cried, "How can you ask me to go?" I almost yelled at her. I was so angry.

"What's wrong? Are you afraid?" she asked, and I felt like she was taunting me. Was I afraid? Where the heck had she been?! Of course I was!

I started to yell and cry, "Yes, I'm afraid. Do you realize that we're fighting cancer right now? Do you know what Bob and I are going through? How can you ask me to do this? Hope, I can't do this, I can't go watch someone die of cancer, I just can't."

She took on a tone of authority, and she raised her voice back at me, "Do you think if you walk away from this it won't still scare you? If you're going to let death scare you so much now, how do you think you're going to fight it? Don't you know that you can't run away from this? When you lie down at night, it will be there; when you wake up, it will be there. You have to face your fear. Don't let fear beat you now, before you've even started." She was right.

I told her that I'd drive her there and maybe go in with her. I hadn't made up my mind yet. I understood what she was saying, and I believed that she was right, but I still didn't know if I could handle it. As we drove, we were both quiet until we pulled up to the hospital. In the parking lot, Hope asked me, "What are you feeling?"

"Empty. I have nothing to give her, Hope, nothing." My words sounded as empty as I felt. I was so panicked I had a hard time walking across the parking lot. We entered the hospice wing and were directed to Sue's room. The minute I walked through the doors, all fear left me. Though I felt so empty on the way, I became so filled with peace when we entered her room. Hope and I sat in the room and prayed for her, held her hands, sang to her. It was the most unbelievable feeling. I lost myself, my fear, my selfishness. I witnessed this most peaceful, joyful, comforting thing. Sue died that day. In death, I found life. I thanked God for His presence. I couldn't believe what had happened to me. At one point in the experience, Hope looked across the bed at me and smiled, "Go look at yourself in the mirror," she said.

She stood behind me as I looked at myself, "You look as if you're almost glowing. You look absolutely beautiful. God is with you." I didn't have to see it; I could feel it.

* * * * * * *

In the next few days, I read a story in the Bible about Gideon. He was facing an enemy, an army. God woke him one night and told him to go into his enemy's camp. Gideon thought this sounded crazy. Go into my enemy's camp? But he did, and he listened. God made Gideon choose a small amount of men to fight the battle with him. God told Gideon that He would be with him. God had Gideon shrink his army so that the army would not be able to boast about their own strength. They would instead give the glory of victory to God. I had been to my enemy's camp. I'd seen death. I began to ask God who would go with me to fight. He was showing me how to choose my warriors.

December 11, 2003:

Judges 7:9 ..the Lord said to Gideon, "Get up, go down against the camp with your servant Purah and listen to what they are saying. Afterward, you will be encouraged to attack the camp. (NIV Bible)

Crazy! Listen to the enemy.

If you are afraid (I was), go and listen (I did); afterward, you will be encouraged to attack the camp. Attack? Is the enemy camping in our household, in Bob? I needed to weed out those who would go with me. Do I depend on, talk to, receive help from only those who will know that this battle will only be won by God? God, all we really need is You. You are our power. After going to the enemy's camp, I felt fear no more. I was encouraged. Do You have an attack for me, God? The enemy is cancer. What is our attack? What is the action You wish me to take?

Insurance still negotiating over money and a contract. Is this the attack? Ask our attorney to pursue this? I don't feel that this is it. Speak, Father.

14
Five Wishes

The hospital offered a BMT caregiver class to ready families for the process of a bone marrow transplant. Bob and I attended and invited my mom and his entire family. We thought that some of their fear would go away if they understood more. I critiqued the class as an oncology nurse. I listened to the dietician, the nurse, the social worker and thought, "This is comprehensive. We should have done this at the cancer center where I worked. This is helpful." I didn't worry about what Bob's family was thinking, about what my mom was thinking, or to be honest, even about what Bob was thinking. I just hoped that it would increase their knowledge and thereby alleviate some fear. I knew how to take care of a BMT patient; I had done so. I didn't want anyone else to help take care of him for fear they would hurt him. I'd take care of him, and they could help me keep the household running. I wouldn't leave him. I couldn't. It was as if I were suffering from separation anxiety.

Unfortunately, I believe that as we listened to the nurse explain what to expect, Bob's family's fear grew. The more information they received, the more scared they became. I hadn't realized how much they didn't understand what was happening. I hadn't realized how much my and my mom's background had prepared us for what was happening. I was confident in my abilities to care for my husband during his transplant. I had no idea what was in store, but I was not afraid of the transplant. I realized what fear could do to someone. I knew I didn't want that fear to come on to me or to Bob, but I didn't understand how to help anyone else.

Their fear and anxiety were so real and so scary to me that I tried to stay as far away from it as possible.

At the time, it seemed to me that the information they gathered was used as ammunition against us. They learned that Bob would have a compromised immune system and decided that they should come and sterilize our house. They learned that he would have special dietary needs after the transplant and decided that they wouldn't cook for him unless we had a menu prepared by a hospital-approved dietician. They learned that he'd need blood and platelet transfusions, and they tried to donate months in advance when it wasn't necessary yet. All positive things. All loving things for a family to do. I couldn't explain to them that we weren't refusing their attempts to help; we were refusing to let fear rule us. We were refusing to act on fear.

We were fighting death. We were fighting on another level. We weren't going to allow every fear and anxiety to change us. We were concentrating on life. We were choosing life. We wouldn't be distracted by every possible side effect, every symptom of the disease or treatment. We had tunnel vision and were looking only for healing. We weren't going to focus on the enemy or anything that he had for us. We were trying as hard as we could to concentrate and keep our eyes fixed on God.

* * * * * * *

One of the pieces of information that we obtained from this class was a "Five Wishes" book. It was for the patient and care giver to complete. It was basically a living will. It was in legal format, and it listed the patient's wishes for care at time of death or near death. It also gave power of attorney to the person that the patient so designated. I filed the booklet away. Why would we need this? Though the form was filed away, the annoying memory of it wasn't. At work one day, I told Paula about the "Five Wishes."

"Can you believe how the enemy is messing with us? They gave us this form to fill out in case Bob is close to death! I'm trying so hard to believe that he's going to be okay and the whole time I have to face death. Why should we prepare for death? He's not dying!" I tried to dismiss the booklet.

Paula asked what the "Five Wishes" were. I explained the concept, but I didn't know all five of them because I hadn't read them. "Basically it is a legal form telling whom he wants to make health care decisions for him if he's unable to make them for himself, and what kind of care he wants if he should need life support measures, which he won't. There is a power of attorney form in the back for him to designate his care taker," I quickly explained it to her. "They want him to complete it before the transplant."

Aimie was home for Christmas vacation and was working in the office with us that day. She listened to our conversation and started to get upset. "Why are you talking about this stuff? He's not going to die. Stop!" She was agitated.

"I know, Aimie, but before he goes into the hospital, they want to cover all of the bases. A transplant is a very serious procedure, and there are very serious potential side effects," I sounded like the oncology nurse again.

"Why do you have to write it down? You're his wife; you're a nurse! You'll take care of him." So simple.

She then yelled into the other room, "Bob! Come here."

Sometimes it is more obvious than others that the girls were raised by Bob, and this was one of those times. Bob is a constant joker, loves to make people laugh, and he likes to lighten the mood in the room. Aimie followed after that sentiment.

As Bob walked into our office, "Bob, you and Mom have to fill out these forms for the hospital. You have to decide and write down who will take care of you when you're sick. Is it okay with you if I manage all of the money while you're sick?"

We all broke out into laughter. Aimie is notorious for being a spender. She's always asking Bob for money, always! Gas money, lunch money, grocery money, school supply money, fun money, etc. Money management has always been a lesson that Bob has struggled to teach Aimie. Their philosophies differed. He saves for a rainy day; she spends rain or shine. The laughter broke the ice, and now Bob wanted to know what we were really talking about. None of us realized how important that moment was. We would need that stupid piece of paper signed. We would need to have Bob's signature on a power of attorney stating his wishes. It would be the only thing that convinced his family to pay any attention to me. I reminded Bob about the "Five Wishes."

"Should we just sign it and get it over with?" I asked.

"Okay, Paula gets the business; Kim, you take care of me; and Aimie gets the money." We all laughed again. How funny that there was a day coming when Paula would be running the business, I would be taking care of Bob, and Aimie would be pilfering through Bob's wallet for gas money. How funny that we laughed then at something that later would be so traumatic.

"Seriously, Bob, who do you want taking care of you if you should get sick enough that you can't take care of yourself?" I ventured into this conversation hesitantly.

"You! Why do you have to ask?!" He seemed agitated with the conversation now that it had turned serious.

"Well, I just wanted to make sure." One more thing. "What if I'm too emotionally crippled to make decisions?" He had always told me that I was too emotional; it was a poke at another joke. I didn't really expect an answer. He answered anyway.

"Your mom. She's a nurse, she's smart, and she'd know what you would want better than anyone else." Paula, Aimie, and I sat there in silence.

Now the conversation was getting too serious for me. We were heading down a road that I didn't want to travel. Conversation over.

"So what are you working on today?" Back to work. I could always find something work-related to talk about when I wanted to change the subject. Paula, Aimie, and I had listened to Bob. We all heard his choices.

We didn't write it down; we didn't have to. We knew Bob, anyone who did would know his choices. We didn't think we'd need it in writing. A few months later, we did. Not only would we write it, we would be asked to drive it to the hospital, immediately.

15
Shutting the Door to Fear

Approximately one week after Sue's death, in late December of 2003, while at work, I received a phone call from our new case manager, "I don't know what's going on, but the medical director of our office just came in and told me to call and have you write a letter explaining why it is so important to you and Bob that you stay in Denver for his transplant. We need it here by tomorrow morning."

I was so excited; I knew I could convince them. It made perfect sense that he stay in Denver. Finally, someone was asking our opinion, and, boy, were they going to get it. I started typing with a vengeance. I was going to tell them a thing or two. This letter *had* to convince them. The pressure was immense.

None of this mattered; what mattered is that God had answered our prayer. He wanted us to stay home. We were "in the right place." As I was proofreading the letter, the perfect letter, and trying to finish it with a line that expressed our desperation without sounding too hopeless, I prayed that God would let this letter do what was intended. I asked Him to please speak for me; I asked him to please speak to the medical director.

As I put the finishing touches and finishing prayers on this letter, the phone rang. It was December 23, 2003 at approximately 4:00 P.M. when the case manager called back. "Mrs. Hritz, I don't understand how or why, but the medical director just walked back into my office and said that I should call and tell you that Bob has a contract at the hospital in Denver. You're staying in Denver for the transplant. Merry Christmas."

I sat in awe for what seemed forever before I spoke, "But I'm not finished with the letter." I hadn't presented my case! I didn't understand.

"I know; we don't need it. You're approved. We'll write a contract for Bob's transplant in Denver." She sounded so happy.

I made her repeat herself, "Say it again."

She did. "Bob's staying in Denver for his transplant; you are staying home."

I laughed out loud and told her that we had been praying for the medical director.

She told me, "Well, it must have worked. Keep praying. I don't know how else to explain this. Merry Christmas, Kim."

What a Christmas gift! Praise God! We were staying home! We were approved for transplant! Merry Christmas indeed.

****

Bob and I were ecstatic! We excitedly told everyone that it was meant to be, we were staying home. We were so ready to start this process, so ready to finish and put this disease and sickness behind us. We felt like the gates had been opened, and it was time to go! Thank You, God! We felt so ready, so taken care of, so confident that God was in control. We knew Bob was going to be okay. No more fear, no more doubt. The whole process seemed miraculous. The negotiators had made an allowance for Bob to have his transplant in Denver without even hearing my arguments. God must have stepped in; it was all the confirmation that we needed. God was showing himself in our battle.

As with Gideon, I began to see the warriors showing themselves, too. I saw those who would go with us, those who would believe with us. I began to see the lines being drawn. It was a bit scary, but I was encouraged by what God was showing me. He was teaching me to pray in ways that I'd never prayed before. The spiritual warfare was becoming more and more evident as the time for transplant grew closer.

Fear and doubt became alive like unwelcome entities, actual intrusive beings into our home. I began to pray that God not allow any unclean or evil spirit to enter our home. I prayed that only God and His presence fill us and our home. I asked Him to clean us of fear, of doubt, of anxiety. I asked that He would fill us with peace and strength. I prayed over our house, and I anointed our doors with oil and spoke out loud that no evil was welcome in our home. No fear, no doubt.

This may sound surreal, or even a bit wacky, but I know it to be true. I know that God was showing me things to help me. I don't know why. I don't know why He allowed me to see this. I only thank Him that He allowed it and that He gave me the courage to understand what I was seeing.

I began to see fear, and I believe I saw it on people. This fear, this entity, used people as a vehicle to try and get to Bob or me. I saw their fear, and I saw what it was doing to them. They were petrified; they were possessed with it. I prayed that God would release them from the fear, but mostly I prayed that the fear would not come upon Bob or me. It was a battle that I fought often. I knew that I could resist the fear with God's help, but I learned that I would have to actively resist, and frequently. I began to blur the lines between the fear and the person to whom it was attached. I was so intent on fighting the fear that I sometimes fought the person.

I remember yelling at my mom when I would see the fear in her. "Don't let this happen to you! We cannot give in!" She often looked at me like I was nuts, but nevertheless, she resisted the fear, and it would flee.

I wish I could have yelled at Bob's family, too, but I was afraid of them. The fear that I saw in them was so real that it scared me. I was petrified of them. I was afraid to talk to them, afraid that they would start to question me again: "Do you think he should see another doctor? Do you think he should be eating that? Do you think he should be going to work? Do you think he should be trying experimental treatments?" The questioning brought so much fear. It opened doors of doubt and through those doors, I found terror. I couldn't even respond to the questions. I must have seemed so rude when I ignored their questions. I can't even imagine what they were thinking of me.

16
With Us or Against Us

Bob's entire family was in Denver for the holidays, and we planned to spend Christmas together with both of our families. The day that we received the good news we called everyone and told them. We decided to meet at a nearby restaurant for dinner. We were celebrating! Upon arriving at the restaurant and finding that the wait was over an hour, I sent Bob, his parents, and my parents to our house to wait and decided that Bob's siblings and I would order take out and bring it back to the house.

While waiting, I realized quickly that I was outnumbered. His two brothers and two sisters did not share in my enthusiasm in finding out that Bob would soon be having his transplant in Denver.

I sat at the table and answered a barrage of fear-filled questions, "Do you think that it's best to have transplant here? Maybe you should keep looking around at other hospitals. We've been educating ourselves on other cancer hospitals and think maybe there are better hospitals out there. Shouldn't he go to the best? What do you know about this doctor? Have you thought about other treatment options?"

Oh, my gosh! Why were they so far behind? We had gone through this two months ago. Why were they not listening?! Were they trying to be difficult? I just didn't understand. Why were they not supporting Bob and me like we'd asked? I became very frank with them. I explained that every time one of them or their parents questioned what we were doing, it scared Bob. I told them that Bob shouldn't be going into transplant with any negative emotions, especially fear. I asked them again to support our decisions. I asked them to please quit doubting everything. I told them that we appreciated their concern, but that they needed to understand that we were moving ahead with the treatment that we, Bob and I, had decided upon. We needed their support. They explained that they were just scared and confused and that their parents were also nervous and wanted to feel confident that we were doing the right thing. I assured them that we were doing what every doctor had recommended; it made medical sense, and we were ready. I agreed with them that this was a very difficult decision and a very fearful time in our lives, but that we truly believed we were in the right place.

I told them about the day that Bob and I prayed before seeing the BMT doctor and had asked God to let us know if we were in the right place. I told them about the nurse who looked Bob in the eyes and used the exact words, "Well, you're in the right place." I don't know that they appreciated my faith; I don't know that they even saw it then. I didn't know where any of them were in their relationships with God; that wasn't a conversation that I'd had with any of them.

We had what I thought was a very good conversation, though. We were open and honest. They were scared; I appreciated that. I asked for their support and for them to please stand with us. They agreed, and I thought it was a great talk. I was excited for their support. We shared a nice evening together.

I look back and wonder what Bob's brothers and sisters got out of that talk. Was I such a bad judge of character that I believed us all to be together on the same team when truly they were not buying a word of what I was saying? Was I not speaking their language? I didn't know how else to ask; I didn't know how else to express what I was feeling. Why did everything turn so sour afterwards? I shared everything that I felt. I opened up completely to them.

I remember one day even telling one of his sisters, "Why are you all trying so hard to make this decision *for* him?"

Before I realized what I was saying, it was out, and she reacted, "Because we love him!"

I knew that. I knew that they loved Bob, and I knew that he loved them. But they weren't acting out of love; they were acting out of fear. Fear!

They said it all of the time. "We're afraid Bob isn't doing the best thing."

Do not be afraid. The Bible taught me to worry about nothing and to pray about everything. Was God forcing me to be sure? Was God requiring me to be so convinced that we were in the right place because I would need that confidence later? Why were we being made to fight so hard to convince his family that we were doing the right thing? Why couldn't we just all agree?

* * * * * * *

Bob and I invited our families over for Christmas Eve. Bob's oldest brother Steve came to me and said, "I'd like to apologize. I didn't realize that we were hurting Bob so much. I heard that he had to take a sleeping pill to get to bed one night after we were trying to get him to find a new doctor. We never meant to hurt him. Next time I do something like that, you can tell me to go to hell." I found it to be a strange choice of words.

I forgave him and explained again that we just really wanted to feel like they were on the same page with us. We just wanted support and encouragement. Bob needed to be as positive and upbeat as possible going into this. His psychological health was very important. Steve agreed.

Later that night Bob pulled me aside and handed me a piece of paper. It had a name and phone number on it. I asked what it was. "When my dad got here, he handed this to me and told me that it was the name and phone number of that doctor in California that Steve had spoken to on the phone. He told me that I should call him. He told me that it wouldn't hurt anything for me to just talk to him."

OH, MY GOSH! I felt like I was going to explode. What did we need to do to get through to them?! How could they allow this fear to be so in control? I handed the piece of paper back to Bob because I didn't even want to touch it. Why? Why were they so relentless? Did they really think that we should go to California for a transplant? Did they think that this doctor had a magic pill that would cure Bob? Did they think that we had to see more doctors to make a decision, or did they just want to be the ones making the decisions?

I didn't know. I really didn't know why they were doing what they were doing. They didn't talk to me about it. They never talked to me about it. They only talked to Bob, and they only talked when I wasn't around. Though it was disguised as a loving family trying to help, I felt that it was a tactic of the enemy: Divide and conquer.

Bob had the paper in his hand. He stared at it, and then looked back at me. He shook his head and made a face, a very sad face. "Why are they doing this to me, Kim?"

I hated what they were doing. I wanted to go kick them all out of my house! How dare they come into our house and bring this doubt and fear again! How dare they completely disregard every request that we had made of them! Stop looking for new doctors! That's all we'd asked! Why couldn't they stop? And now Bob was asking me why they were doing this? How should I know? I wanted to ask them, I wanted to go straight into the other room and ask them.

"Let's go ask them why they're doing it!"

Maybe it was the anger in my voice that snapped Bob out of his sadness. "No! I'll just throw it away and ignore it. I'll just keep ignoring them. They can do whatever they want to me; I won't let it hurt me anymore."

Great! Bob was still going to continue to let this fear beat him down while he was battling cancer. Great strategy. He was saying, "I can fight my family's fear AND the cancer, too." No big deal. Not a very good battle plan if you ask me. Why wouldn't he just stand up to them? What was so hard about Bob standing up to his parents? Why couldn't he just tell them to stop?

Bob wouldn't allow me to talk to his parents that night. He wouldn't let me talk to them the next day, either. I asked if we could sit down with them and calmly explain why we didn't want them to suggest new doctors. Surely, they would understand. Bob refused. "They'll stop. They just have to do this. This is what they do. I don't understand it either, but they think they know best. They just want it their way; they'll get over it." I wish I would have insisted that we talk to them. I wish I would have begged Bob, I wish I would have even talked to his parents without his permission, but I didn't. Things could have been so different.

17
Bob's Nadir

We made an appointment with the BMT doctor again. We were ready to go. He agreed that the steroids had taken a toll on Bob and that we should get to transplant as soon as possible. What was not said, but understood by all, was that "Now that the insurance has approved your treatment, and we know we will be paid, we can get started." Nevertheless, we were happy to get going. He drew blood and prepared Bob for a few doses of outpatient high dose chemotherapy to clean his body of the cancer. The steroids had helped, but the cancer was still there. In order for Bob to donate his own stem cells for the transplant, they would have to be cancer-free. They weren't yet, so we prepared for his first chemotherapy. We went to the hospital and had a PIC line, an intravenous line that stays in for an extended period of time, placed in his right arm. The line would be used for blood draws and chemotherapy infusions. He would have the line placed in the morning of January 5, 2004, and then we'd go straight to the cancer center for his chemo. Everything was planned. We were both very calm and ready to get started.

We decided to go to the cancer center alone. Family members offered to come; we politely refused and said we'd be fine. We knew it would be a long scary day and felt that adding anyone else would only add to our stress. We didn't worry about hurting anyone's feelings; this was about us.
I began to speak for Bob, and speak as if we were one. "We're here for chemo. We're getting a PIC line placed today. We'll need some anti-emetics in case we get sick."

It was a little weird, I guess, but Bob said, "You're going through this as much as I am."

It was so strange to watch the I.V. bags go up, so strange to listen to the nurses check the doses and the bags in front of us, so clinical, so foreign. Wow. Bob's having chemotherapy. I was happy to know that I knew about Cytoxan, the drug that he was taking, but on the other hand, I was wishing I didn't know what I did. I wanted the nurses and the doctors to tell us everything as they would to any other patient.

"Assume I know nothing," I would tell them. After all, in the mental state I was in, I probably could have used a few refresher courses. The day went very well. We were both very calm.

January 5, 2004:

At hospital waiting for Bob to have his PIC line placed. First PIC line then chemotherapy. Cytoxan 3 gm/m^2, Mesna, and I.V. fluids. He'll also be restaged today. Restaged to see if the Decadron worked. It's definitely had an effect on Bob. Side effects have been severe. He's gained thirty pounds and lost most of it, too. On some weekends, a nineteen-pound weight gain is not uncommon. His body doesn't look the same. Sometimes I can ignore this disease, then I see him step out of the shower – ouch! I don't care about his physical appearance so much; I just see the effect on his body and realize that he's sick. Not the same. Not my Bob. It's okay, he'll be better.

* * * * * * *

I stayed home from work with Bob for the first few days. I kept him on anti-nausea medication around the clock. I forced him to drink fluids but knew not to force him to eat. He had two days of nausea and diarrhea and a few times of vomiting, but for the most part, he sailed through. I was so happy with his tolerance of the treatment that I decided to go to work one day in the middle of the week. I called his parents and asked if they'd come sit with him. They obliged. Bob slept on the couch most of the day. I called to check on him often.

January 7, 2004:

Chemotherapy was Monday. Today is Wednesday. The peace that God has given me is unbelievable. Bob and I had a good night; he was up a few times with diarrhea but no vomiting. He's been on Ativan every six hours and is very sleepy. Vomited this morning once after taking his blood pressure medication. I've asked his parents to come and sit with him while I go to work for the day. It is good to get out. I feel like it's a way to stay me. I can get very protective and territorial with him. Sometimes I feel like I have to protect him, and I can't get away from him. When I do get away, it makes me feel a little better. It's hard to get to the away part. Life is for the living and we ARE living. I have to remember to spend time living and not dying.

Rational, logical thought. Optimistic vs. pessimistic. Flesh vs. Spirit. Face the facts. Speak the word. Speak to the illness. Cancer, myeloma, you are not welcome here. You were not invited; you must go. By the power of the blood, the shed blood, the blood of Jesus Christ of Nazareth, cancer must flee. Resist the enemy, and he must flee. Enemy, I speak to you by the power of the Risen One. Go! Leave! Get out and don't come back. The word of God says if I ask and believe in my heart, I can receive what I ask. I am asking. My request is in line with the word and will of my God. Health, Healing. By the power of the blood. "Not by might, not by power, but by my Spirit," says the Lord.

Every time I feel like I need to understand what's going on here and speak that Bob has myeloma – cancer – that this is serious and that he is fighting for his life, I feel later that this disease is getting to me. It's trying to get me comfortable with it here in my house and lull me into giving in, into accepting it.

It's a fight for life; we're fighting death. We are fighting death. Accept that whatever happens, happens. Who can know the mind of God? How dare I tell God the outcome? This is God's decision. He knows my heart, knows my wish, knows my desire. I want Bob to live; I would do anything to make it so, but it's God's decision, and I will love God no matter what happens. I want Bob to live, but if God has a plan for the greater good, that requires that Bob not live... who am I to argue with God? Who am I to tell God to change the big plan because of my feelings?

Okay, that's one minute and the next... I'll tell you who I am! I am a child of God. A child of the King! And I ask, no beg, my Father in heaven...please, God, take this enemy out of our lives. Give us the victory over our enemy. Give us healing that Jesus died for. The victory that Jehosophat had. Your battle, Lord.

YOURS. And You give us the victory. Ask and we shall receive. ONLY BELIEVE. Healing in His wings. Cancer has no place here. No place. Resisted, must flee. Greater is He my Lord who is in me, in Bob, than the enemy of the world. No place here. Flee. We walk by faith. We walk by faith.

The next journal entry would be January 16, 2004. It would read "Friday… what a week… what a God we serve… what a…"

The week that I referred to was January 12th through the 16th. The week is somewhat of a blur.

By Sunday, the 11th, six days after his chemo, Bob was feeling well enough to get up and around and was eating again. I was amazed at how well he had done. His parents had decided to go home to St. Louis to gather more household goods for their apartment; they were going to leave on Monday, seven days after the chemotherapy. They invited Bob over for dinner on Sunday, and they wanted to be alone with him. Therefore, I decided to go out with my brother, Stan, and his girlfriend, Lisa.

Lisa and Stan had been together for quite a while. She was like part of the family. I assumed that they would be together forever. High intensity stress does funny things to a relationship. She was a physician's assistant and was very helpful when Bob became sick. She was there with us through every bit of diagnosis; she helped my mother and I brainstorm through the denial process. When she saw Bob, she asked how he was feeling in a more clinical way than most. She diagnosed symptoms and offered suggestions for the alleviation of discomfort. She listened to me and gave support. She truly cared. Not just for Stan's sake, but for ours. We loved her.

One day while Lisa's normal life was be-bopping along, she received a phone call from her father back home in Washington, D. C. Lisa's mother had been in a car accident and was in the E.R. She had x-rays taken as a result of the accident, and the x-rays showed that she had tumors in her lungs and brain—metastatic cancer. Lisa's family would be starting their battle against cancer and death. It seemed unfair. Lisa would be taken away from us, taken away from Stan to go across country to fight a battle of her own.

She left shortly after finding out the news. She would be staying in D. C. for the next few months to help to care for her mother. There would be chemotherapy and radiation therapy. Lisa would become her mom's primary caretaker. Lisa was a lot like me at that time. She assumed the role that she knew she must, with a vengeance. She was determined to be the best caretaker daughter she could. She was angry, sad, confused, but determined. She made the only choice that she could possibly make: She left Denver and moved to D. C. Stan and she tried to maintain their relationship across country and during the turmoil that was now life to both of them. He fought a battle in two states. He would support me and our family here, then fly to D. C. to help Lisa cope with her life in D.C.. He racked up frequent flyer miles, dwindled his vacation time to nothing, and generally caught himself coming and going.

One week, Lisa, needing a break from her caregiver role, decided to come home to Denver for a weekend.

Bob was doing wonderfully and since he was going to see his parents, I figured it wouldn't hurt for me to go out with Stan and Lisa. I told Bob to call when he was coming home, and I'd meet him. Stan picked me up, and we went out. I felt like I was playing hooky. I was leaving him alone with his parents.

They weren't really the enemy, and they seemed like they were more and more supportive of our decisions as of late. They wouldn't fill him with doubt, fear, and anxiety now. Besides, I needed to be away. I needed this.

Lisa, Stan, and I had dinner. Lisa and I began to compare and contrast our roles. We complained really. We complained like spoiled, selfish brats. We were tired. It was unfair that our lives had turned into what they had. We didn't want to do what we were doing, didn't want our loved ones to be sick anymore. We were sick of cancer and what it had already stolen from our lives. We were coping. It felt good to have someone else agree with me, to have someone who knew what I was saying, someone else who had a loved one whom they completely loved, unconditionally loved, and yet at the same time were tired of. We both had the same feelings.

"My mom should be taking care of me!" Lisa exclaimed. Likewise, Bob should be my caretaker. In the end, we knew that we wouldn't have it any other way. There were so many similarities in what we were going through. No one else could care for Lisa's mom the way she could; I was that person for Bob. Lisa wouldn't trust anyone else to make the decisions that she was making, same for me. She was familiar with a hospital routine and felt comfortable talking with the doctors and nurses. We hugged, vented to each other, cried with each other; we understood each other. More than anything, I think, we built each other up. We strengthened each other for what was to come. That evening would be the last night that Lisa and I had a real conversation. We started in such similar places, and over the next few months would end up on what seemed like other sides of the world.

Bob called to let me know that he was home and told me that he was very cold and was going to bed. I told him that I would have Stan and Lisa bring me back, but that he should ask Katie to lie down next to him and keep him warm. He said he would. I called Katie and told her to go ask Bob if he needed anything. She said that he was crying and told her that he loved her. I came home immediately.

Stan and Lisa came in. It was early. Bob was upstairs in bed, and I went to check on him. He was falling asleep but told me that he didn't feel well. I asked him to be more specific. He couldn't. "I just don't feel right; I don't know." I asked if he were upset.

He said, "No, it's more like… I don't know, maybe I'm just tired. My left leg keeps feeling like it's falling asleep, but not really."

Okay, left leg falling asleep. I had no idea what that meant but went through a quick assessment in my mind. Numbness and tingling, either neurological or circulatory. I asked him to stand up for me; he did. I asked him to walk, he did. I asked him to touch his finger tips to his nose, he did. I asked him to squeeze my hands, look into my eyes, smile, stick his tongue out. All fine. I felt his left leg in comparison to his right leg. Warm, color same. I performed the Holman sign, by pushing his toes up toward his head to assess for pain, which would indicate a blood clot in his leg. No pain.

"When did this start? Is it continuous?" He assured me that it was no big deal, and he just needed to go to sleep as he was very tired from his outing.

"Maybe I just laid on it weird," he said.

I asked him if it would be okay if Lisa assessed him. He thought I was overreacting but agreed. She came upstairs and asked a bunch of questions, had him repeat the quick neurological test that I'd just performed. Everything seemed fine, nothing to worry about. Bob said that he was okay and just wanted to sleep. We left him alone and went back downstairs. It is amazing how quickly Lisa and I went from whining and feeling sorry for ourselves to the roles that we had learned to assume: caretaker, and not just caretaker, medical professionals. But all of the training and professionalism in the world couldn't have prepared us for what was to come. We continued to go upstairs and check on Bob every thirty minutes until she and Stan left at around midnight. Bob was fine. Lisa was leaving in the morning to go back to D. C. We hugged good bye and encouraged each other. We exchanged cell phone numbers and promised to call each other for support along the way, but neither of us called.

18
Unloading Only

Before going to bed, I woke Bob again; he was fine. I fell asleep, content in knowing that we would be seeing Dr. Jeffries in the morning, and he would be able to assess Bob, draw blood, and ease the fear that was creeping in.

We didn't make it to the doctor's office the next morning, though. Bob woke up early, around 7:00 A.M. He paced back and forth next to the bed.

"Kim, my leg feels weird again, and so does my left arm. I can't explain it." That was it; we were going to Dr. Jeffries' office early. I called the cancer center and told them that we had a one o'clock appointment scheduled, but I wanted to bring him in early due to this weird feeling he was having. They said to come right in.

Bob and I dressed, threw on sweat pants and tee shirts, didn't even shower. I was starting to freak out a bit. I couldn't piece together what was happening. Why was he feeling weird in his left arm and leg? What was this indicative of? We would not soon find out.

I drove to the clinic and talked to Bob the entire time, questioning him. He was answering questions and communicating well, didn't seem to be in any pain, but stated that he just felt weird and couldn't explain how. When I was a nurse, I can remember taking care of patients who told me that they'd felt "weird" or "funny." It had been my experience that those were the ones you have to watch out for. Vague symptoms were hard to diagnose. Everything that happened to Bob over the next few months would be hard to figure out; nothing seemed to be fixable. I was totally losing control.

We were just five minutes or so from the doctor's office when I looked over at Bob while he was talking and noticed that the left side of his cheek seemed to be twitching. I told him to stop. He pulled the visor down, looked into the mirror and said, "Huh. That's weird. I can't control it." I immediately grabbed for my purse because I needed my phone, and I needed help NOW. Bob was having a seizure. I knew it; I saw it. I started to reach into the backseat for the bag that contained my day planner with the doctor's phone number in it. Bob asked what I was doing. "What do you need? Keep your eyes on the road, Kim, I'll get it." He sounded so normal, but his left cheek was now contorting a bit so that the left side of his mouth was turning upward into a smile.

"Get my bag, NOW!" I yelled. He knew only by what he was seeing in me that something was wrong.

"Kim, what's going on?" He sounded scared.

"Do you feel okay?" I asked, ignoring his question.

"Yes, my leg feels like it may be getting a little worse, though, like I need to stand up and walk on it. It feels asleep, but not tingly." I was opening my day timer with my right hand, flipping through to the phone numbers, and holding my phone and steering wheel with my left. "Kim, why don't you let me find the number you're looking for?"

"It's okay, I have it. Fix your face, Bob." He pulled the visor down again and rubbed his left cheek. I just wanted him to wipe it away. If I didn't have to see it, it wasn't happening.

I found the number, dialed the clinic, and told the first nurse who answered that we were going straight to the emergency room. I told her what was happening, and she agreed. She said she'd tell Dr. Jeffries and he'd call the E.R. staff to order some tests.

We pulled into the short term parking marked "Unload Only," and I jumped out and circled the front of the car. Bob was slowly getting out of the car on his side. We walked slowly to the entrance with my arm around his waist. My heart was beating so fast I felt like I was running. We met the triage nurse at the front desk, and I told her that my husband was having numbness in his left leg, and I thought he had just had a seizure in the car.

Bob looked at me very surprised, "What?" I squeezed him around the waist and told him it would be okay. He looked so confused. The nurse quickly rose to her feet, grabbed a wheelchair that was sitting next to a set of double doors, asked Bob to sit down, and took him through those doors.

I started to follow, and she said over her shoulder, "Can you fill out his paperwork first? The window to the left." Damn insurance again.

My husband just had what I was convinced was a seizure and was being whisked away by a stranger who wouldn't even let me cross through the doors until I filled out the paperwork for payment. I felt like throwing my purse through the window and making a run for it before the doors closed. I didn't. I sat down in a chair across a desk that was surrounded in glass and waited. I waited! They weren't even ready. The woman was on the phone. What was she talking about? It couldn't have been more important than what I needed! Hang up already, stop making me wait! I considered getting up and going in to see Bob. Damn her! If she wanted my insurance card so badly, she would have hung up the phone. I started to count in my head. How high would I get before I would just get up: 41, 42, 43, 44? My knees were bouncing up and down; my fingers were tapping the insurance card that I was holding against the wallet sitting open in my lap. 45, 46, 47, 48. I'm not going to sit here long. 49, 50, 51, 52. It hadn't even been one minute yet, but it seemed like an eternity. The woman hung up the phone, thank God!

She stood up, "I'll be right with you." She said very politely and a little too calmly for my liking, and she disappeared. 53, 54, 55, 56. Why wasn't anyone as freaked out as I was? For God's sake, my husband could be back there having a seizure for all I knew! Where was she? 57, 58, 59, 60. That was it; I was going to find Bob. They knew where to find me. I stood up and looked for the button on the wall that would open the double doors, and they opened on their own. A man in scrubs walked through them. "Are you Kim Hritz?"

"Yes."

"Hi, I'm taking care of Bob, and we have some questions. Can you come back and help him answer them?" Thank God!

"Yes." I was walking through the doors without filling out my paperwork. Ahhh! Bob was on a stretcher, already in a hospital gown. He looked fine, and when he saw me he said, "You'll have to answer these questions. I don't know the names of all the drugs that I've been on."

I smiled at him because he seemed like the same impatient man whom I'd married. He seemed slightly irritated with the details, as usual. He knew my job was to handle the paperwork, so he didn't even mess with it.

The nurse started with, "So you're here because your husband is feeling weird, has some strange numbness in his left leg, and had some facial twitching in the car." I agreed, and he continued with the history and physical questions. I answered them and explained everything in detail that had happened over the past six to eight hours and six months.

He was satisfied with the assessment and said that the doctors would be right in, and tests were already ordered. "What tests?" I asked.

They would start with blood work and an MRI of his head. They'd be here to get him shortly.

I called my mom and told her that we were in the E.R., that Bob had had a seizure, and to please come. She said she'd be right there. The woman from the other side of the double doors came to me and asked for Bob's insurance card and a few signatures. I knew she'd find me. I called Bob's brother Dave and told him what had happened and that we didn't know anything yet. He informed me that Bob's parents had just left that morning to drive back to St. Louis to pick up more household goods for their apartment. They weren't expected back for at least a week.

"Should I call them? I don't want to worry them," he said.

I don't know what I answered exactly. I think I told him that he would have to make that decision on his own. Next I called Stan. He was taking Lisa to the airport but would be there shortly. I had called the three people whom I knew I must. Were they the warriors that were being called to go with us?

I waited with Bob for the tech to come and get him for the MRI. He said that he felt about the same, no better, no worse. He didn't seem worried at all. I was a nervous wreck. Why was he having seizures? What kind of reaction to high-dose Cytoxan was this? I couldn't sit still; I paced. He lay on the stretcher with his legs crossed at the ankles with his hands crossed on his stomach. He looked as if he were lying on the couch watching television, very relaxed. How could he be sick? He told me to calm down.

"It'll be okay; this is just a little bump in the road. No big deal. We'll get through it."

He joked about something; I remember his trying to make me laugh. I don't remember what he said, just that I was wondering if he knew how serious this could be. Was he joking to try to calm me or himself? He started to say something and began to make that funny half smile again.

"Bob!" I started to raise my voice; he was having another seizure. The seizure got worse, I screamed louder. "Help!! Someone help us!"

Within seconds the room was full of nurses and doctors. Bob was having a grand mal seizure. His head started jerking, his arms and legs stiffened, and he began to convulse. His eyes rolled back in his head, and his mouth contorted. It seemed to last forever. One of the nurses was yelling out the actual time that it was lasting.

"30 seconds!" she yelled. The second hand on her watch must have been broken! They lowered the head of his bed, pushed pillows between him and the hand rails, and grabbed an oral airway to shove down his throat. I stood at the foot of his bed and watched in disbelief; my hands up covering my mouth, tears streaming down my cheeks. What was happening?

Oh, God, help us. Oh, God, what's going on here? I was numb. I was scared, confused. I couldn't formulate a thought, much less a sentence. My mom showed up, and I don't even remember what I said to her. I paced back and forth and mumbled something. The nurses and doctors decided to call and speed up the MRI. They told us that we would be going down for it momentarily. I called my brother Stan again, and he told me that he'd be there as soon as he could. I felt like I needed reinforcements.

Bob was resting on the stretcher, with the oral airway still in his mouth. He started to spit it out, so I pushed it back in. He lifted his hand and pulled it out of his mouth. He became alert again but looked very sleepy. The seizure had taken a lot out of him. I stood next to the stretcher, leaned over him, and talked very softly to him. "Bob, do you remember anything that just happened? Do you know that you just had a big seizure?" I asked, trying to sound calm.

"I remember feeling like I needed to spit out my gum, and my mouth wouldn't work. Then I just remember all kinds of doctors and nurses around me. What happened?"

I explained it just as I had seen it and told him that we needed to pray. I laid my head on his chest and prayed.

I cried to God, "Please help us, Father, we're scared. Please let the doctors find what's causing this and help them to make it go away. Jesus please be with us now; we need You." I told Bob to keep his mind on Jesus, and I asked him to please trust God. He told me that he would.

A team of young doctors came in the room: Tim, Joey, and Jeff. They were very young looking: an intern, resident, and medical student. They were part of the medical team at the hospital and were called in to assess Bob. They did a very thorough job and said that they'd wait for the MRI results. Dr. Jeffries had been called and would be over to see Bob shortly.

The orderly was in to take Bob, and my mother and I followed closely. The hallways seemed so long, the elevators so slow. While in the elevator with him, he asked me if my car was still parked in the thirty minute lot. So like Bob! He told me to go move it while he was getting the MRI. I laughed at him and told him that they could tow it as far as I was concerned; I wasn't leaving him.

We reached the radiology department, a place that we would visit at least a dozen times over the next two months, and waited for the technician to come and take him in. We filled out paperwork, assured them that Bob didn't have any metal shavings in his eyes or any metal prosthesis, and the he was good to go. They took him in and told us to wait.

Wait. Such a simple work. Wait. They throw that word around so much in the hospital. Wait for results, wait for someone to come and take you somewhere, wait for a doctor, wait for your husband right here, wait for the pharmacy, wait for the respiratory therapist, wait, wait, wait. God knows that I'm not a very patient person. Most people who know me, do, too. I learned patience. I had to. I waited. While we were waiting, Stan arrived. My mom was so impressed that he had found us. "How did you know where we were? I can't believe you found us!"

"They told me in the emergency room. Where is he?" He sounded impatient. He just wanted to see him, to know that he was okay.

"He's getting his MRI; he'll be out in a minute," I said. We sat in the waiting room. It was small, with ten small chairs and two small tables. There was a large clock on the wall which had a second hand that moved almost as slowly as the one on the watch that the nurse in the E.R. wore. So slowly. I waited. I wondered how this was happening. I couldn't figure it out. A seizure. What did this mean?

Stan is an engineer. Engineers want to figure everything out, maybe in order to fix things, maybe just so they know everything. It was the way Stan's brain worked. He had to understand what was happening; he had to understand what a seizure was. I listened to my mom talk about electrical impulses in the brain, seizure activity, and the possible adverse results from having a seizure.

"But it's possible that he won't have any residual damage from the seizure, right?" Stan asked.

"It depends on what is causing the seizure," she answered.

"So really the seizure is just a symptom of something going wrong in his brain?"

My mom shrugged and gave a half-hearted yes.

Stan asked, "So what is causing the seizure?"

"We don't know, that's why they're doing the MRI, to look at his brain," my mom finished. He was appeased. He would wait for the results with us.

I learned to appreciate Stan's straight-to-the-point questions. He didn't beat around the bush; he didn't have any preconceived motives. He just simply wanted all the facts as we knew them and wanted them as succinctly as possible. He always seemed to be the least emotional when he was gathering facts. It was similar to watching someone put together a jigsaw puzzle. He looked for the right pieces of information, twisted the pieces until they fit into his existing knowledge base, and constructed the picture. He then sat back and took it all in. He knew at this point that all of the pieces weren't available yet. We would wait for them.

When Bob came out of the MRI, they pushed his stretcher up against the wall, and told us they'd call a dispatch person to come and wheel him back to the E.R. Stan asked if he could push him. They told us it was against policy, and we'd have to wait for dispatch. We waited. Bob talked to Stan, and I think it made Stan feel better to see him. He looked like Bob, talked like Bob, just wore a hospital gown and was lying on a stretcher.

When the dispatch orderly showed up, Stan and I looked at each other and smiled. She was a tiny black woman, approximately sixty years old with legs that looked to be no bigger around than broom handles. And they wouldn't let Stan push the stretcher! This is what we were waiting for. Her name tag read Savannah, and during the next two months, Savannah would push Bob all over that hospital. She had strength beyond what her physical appearance let on.

Stan asked, "Can I help you push?"

"Oh, I'll be okay," she said with a confident smile, like she'd been asked that question before.

When we arrived back in the E.R., we thanked her. "Thank you, Savannah."

"You're welcome. Good luck." I think she meant it.

We weren't in the E.R. very long before they had given us a room number. Bob would be going to the third floor, oncology. (Oncology floor?! Why did it still seem so strange to me that he had cancer?) We followed another dispatch person as he pushed Bob up to the third floor.

"Are you going to move your car?" Bob asked me again. Again I told him that I wasn't going to leave him.

We arrived on the oncology floor. As far as hospitals go, it was beautiful and brand new. We were placed in a room at the end of the hall directly across from a waiting room that was furnished with two couches, several comfortable chairs, and a television. I never had a chance to count the chairs. I was too consumed with what would happen to Bob across the hall in his room. His brothers showed up shortly after we arrived, and they looked extremely nervous.

We were still waiting for results from the MRI. We all waited: Bob, me, my mom, Stan, Dave, and Steve. We took turns pacing. We called other family members just to tell them that we didn't yet know anything. Bob flipped through the channels on the television and complained that he hadn't eaten all day. Stan went down to the cafeteria to get him something to eat. I called the nurse and asked if it would be okay to feed Bob. They said they'd have to call and ask one of the doctors. We waited to see if Bob could eat.

I realized that it was getting dark outside. It was evening, and I was still in sweat pants and hadn't showered all day. I couldn't believe that the morning had turned to evening so quickly. I also remembered that my car was still in the E.R. parking lot. I remembered because Bob asked me yet again, "Are you going to move your car?" Steve offered to move it for me. I gave him the key and told him where to find it. He asked where to park it, and I told him that I really didn't know. He said he'd remember and give me directions to find it later.

All of us were waiting, trying to find something to do to ease our minds. Where were the doctors? At least Bob was awake, alert, walking and talking, even complaining about being hungry. Things seemed normal, except for the fact that we were in a hospital room on an oncology floor waiting for MRI results to tell us why Bob was having seizures. Normal had changed.

* * * * * * *

I called and talked to Katie, told her that Paula would stay with her tonight, and I would be staying at the hospital.

She seemed very quiet; I knew she was scared. I also knew that I couldn't comfort her at that point. Paula would be good for her. Katie was so like Paula. They would get through this night together just fine. I tried calling Aimie, but she didn't answer. I left a very normal message on her machine.

"Hi, Aim, it's mom. Just want to talk to you. Could you please call me as soon as you get this message? Love you."

That sounded benign enough. She wouldn't detect any fear in that. Why should I scare her? There was nothing to worry about. I just wanted to tell her that we were in the hospital and ask her to pray. Aimie was a good prayer. It also felt somewhat unfair that she didn't know what was going on yet. She needed to know.

Dave and Steve were still talking about whether or not to tell Bob's mom and dad what had happened. I didn't give an opinion; they knew their parents better than I, and it should have been their decision. Eventually, they decided to call them. We let Bob talk to them to let them hear his voice and be reassured by hearing him. He told them that he'd be okay. I don't know that they realized how serious his condition was; I don't know that Dave and Steve knew how to tell them.

Within the next forty-eight hours, they would know. We would all know.

Stan arrived back in the room with a bacon cheeseburger for Bob. He placed it on the over-bed table and pulled the table up to Bob. Bob began to unwrap the burger before I could stop him.

"Bob, you can't eat until we get permission from the doctor," I told him, only half believing that would stop him from eating.

"Then go get the doctor! I'm hungry!"

I went to the nurses' station and asked if they had orders for Bob yet. They didn't. I asked if they could please call and just get diet orders; otherwise, Bob was going to eat the bacon cheeseburger that he had just unwrapped. They paged Dr. Trevor, a neurologist. He told them that Bob would have to be NPO (nothing by mouth) for twenty-four hours after the seizure. It was standard of care for seizure patients. Seizure patients? Bob wasn't a seizure patient; he was just Bob who happened to have a seizure, and who, by the way, was now a patient. And on the oncology floor on top of that! Ouch!

I went back to tell Bob that he couldn't eat the cheeseburger that he'd already taken a bite of. Stan had gotten enough food for me, too. I hadn't even realized that I hadn't eaten. I took a few bites of a pizza. Dave and Steve split the rest of Bob's cheeseburger. Everyone stayed until Bob fell asleep, and I spent the night at his bedside in a recliner.

19
Heavenly Reinforcements

Tuesday morning came, and I felt like I hadn't really slept. Dr. Jeffries came in to see Bob, took one look at me, and told me to go home and get some rest. I told him I wanted to wait until we had some test results, some answers, but he had none. I glanced at myself in the mirror and saw the reason why he was trying to send me home: I looked even worse than I felt—dried mascara in lines down my face and hair that looked like a rat's nest. I decided to call my mom to have her come up and sit with Bob so that I could run home and get cleaned up. I knew he'd be safe with her.

The doctors kept coming in and asking the same questions. They would hold up a pen, "What is this, Bob?" Point to their watch, "And this?" "What year is it, Bob?" "Who is the president?"

Always the same questions.

Not always the same answers. He went from answering correctly but very slowly, to answering incorrectly, to answering with incoherent words, to not answering at all.

I left and returned as soon as I could, and by that time, Bob was going down for another MRI. "You stay here and get some rest," my mom told me. "Sit in the recliner and sleep. Don't worry; I'll be with him the whole time." I didn't argue with her; I was too exhausted. She turned the light out in the room as she left. Just as I closed my eyes, I heard someone enter the room. It was a woman from the hospital's pastoral care department. She introduced herself as Dee.

"Hello," I hoarsely responded.

"I'm here to talk with you about the grieving process."

"No, not a good time. I'm really tired, and I have to sleep while they're gone."

She kept talking, asking lots of questions. I was so tired I couldn't keep my eyes open.

"Really, I'm too tired now," I pleaded with her.

The questions continued. "Do you have children? How are they handling this?"

What?! How are they handling what? The fact that the only father that they've ever really known has been diagnosed with incurable cancer and now has had a seizure and possibly a stroke that has left him unable to communicate or care for himself? How do you think?!

"They're fine," I responded.

I didn't want to let her into my life. I didn't know her. She kept talking. What was she saying? I remember thinking, "I'm so tired. Would it be rude if I fell asleep while she talked?" As I laid my head back and closed my eyes, I heard Stan walk into the room.

"Kim, where's Bob?" He said, sounding a bit nervous.

Dee held out her hand to him, "Hi, I'm Dee with pastoral care. I'm speaking with Kim about grieving."

Stan practically fell back against the wall as I sat up quickly and yelled, "No!"

"Where is Bob?!" Stan raised his voice over mine.

"MRI with Mom," I instantly replied, trying to calm him.

All color had left his face. Stan immediately lost all confidence in Dee's abilities to help any of us through what was happening. He slowly recovered while she apologized for scaring him. Stan politely but firmly told Dee that we did not need to speak about grieving, because we were believing for a miracle. He then told her that I looked like I needed the rest and told her to leave. She did so and told me that she would be back. God had picked a good warrior to stand beside me. Stan was there so much that I don't know when he slept. Maybe he, like me, didn't.

Mom and Bob came back to the room. Bob was no better. No one had any answers. It was so frustrating. I trusted God still.

Dave and his wife, Andrea, showed up that evening, and Bob didn't remember who Andrea was. She hid behind Dave and cried. Bob's mental status was very hit-and-miss. One minute he'd say a completely coherent sentence, the next he'd jumble sounds together into incomprehensible noises. When this happened, he would look at me with such bewilderment because he knew he wasn't making sense. I always responded in the same way, "It's okay, Bob. It'll be okay." All we did was sit by and watch him slowly but steadily lose his ability to talk or communicate.

Early Wednesday morning was the last time that Bob would communicate with me for the next month. He woke in the middle of the night sporadically and would speak clearly, "Kim, I think I have to go to the bathroom. Can you help me with this IV machine?" As I pulled the blankets off of him, I noticed that he had been incontinent. He just looked at me with the weirdest expression.

"Did I do that?" he asked.

"Yes, Bob, it's okay though. I'll help you."

"I don't…uh…" The expression on his face said it all; he had no idea what was happening. "I'm sorry."

"Don't be; it's okay." I walked him to the bathroom and helped him clean up and change.

I woke Stan, who was sleeping in the waiting room, to help me change the bed linens and put Bob back to bed. A few hours later, Bob woke again, "Kim…"

"What do you need, Bob?"

Just a blank stare this time, and he pointed down between his legs and tried to pull the covers off.

"Wait, I'll help. Do you have to go to the bathroom?" No answer; he just started to get out of bed and pulled at his IV lines. He was acting confused. "No, Bob, stop! Wait for me to help you." I pushed the nurses' call light.

"Can I help you?" The voice from the nurses' station came across the speaker. "I need help, please." I was afraid that he would hurt himself getting out of bed. He was determined to move faster than was safe. The nurse came in, and I explained, "He's been incontinent a few times tonight. He's talking less and less. I need to get him cleaned up. Can you help change his bed, please? Stay with him while I get my brother."

I went to the waiting room again. "Stan, I need your help." I started to cry but stopped myself. What good would that do? Bob needed me. We got a new gown and some towels and took Bob into the bathroom. Stan helped me shower him and clean the floor of stool.

While Stan was in the bathroom helping Bob to shower, Bob spoke, "I think I shit myself."

Stan laughed and replied, "Yes, you did."

Bob shook his head, "What the hell's going on?"

I don't know why he laughed; don't know why it seemed funny. Maybe the lack of sleep, maybe it was a sentence that seemed so "Bob" at the moment. We didn't laugh for long. As we helped dry Bob and put a clean gown on him, the nurse changed his bed linens. We walked Bob back into his bed and positioned his I.V. pole, plugged it in, and I tried to get him to sit down. He wouldn't. I wondered if he were confused again.

"Bob, you need to get back in bed now. It's time to go to bed; it's late." He just stared at me. I put my hands on his shoulders and attempted to gently coax him to get into bed. He didn't budge.

"Bob, what do you want? Do you have to go to the bathroom again?" He just stared at me. "What, Bob? What do you want; can you talk to me?" I stood face to face with him. I was tired, scared, and feeling lost. He looked me in the eyes and brought his left hand up and cupped my right cheek in it. He smiled the saddest smile I've ever seen. I began to cry. "I know, Bob, I know. It's going to be okay. I love you, too."

A tear rolled down his cheek, but he remained silent. He couldn't say it, but he didn't have to say a word. His eyes said it all. He was sorry. He was sorry that he was sick. He was sorry that I was taking care of him. He was sorry for what was happening. So was I. I hugged him, and he hugged me back. I tried to keep myself together. It was a moment that lasted forever. I helped him back into bed and walked out into the hall and cried. It was so very sad for me to know that he was sorry. I went out into the hall and broke down into Stan's arms. I was so scared.

That night, or early morning, was also the time that I witnessed something that brought me both fear and great hope. I saw angels. Maybe they knew it was time to come.

I had pulled myself together, sent Stan back to his waiting room to sleep, and taken my position in the recliner at Bob's bedside. The recliner was facing the same direction as the hospital bed. I had pushed it up alongside Bob so that I could be close to him while we slept. I was playing a worship cassette tape that was mostly piano music. Bob loved listening to piano music; it was very soothing. The cassette I had would run for approximately thirty minutes on each side. During the thirty minutes of music, I would sleep, but when the tape ended, the "click" woke me. I would lean over and back to open the tape deck, turn the tape over, and press "play" again.

During one of my tape changes, I noticed movement out of the corner of my eye. I looked back toward the head of Bob's bed and saw the most awesome sight I've ever laid eyes on. To this day I have never again seen such a magnificent sight.

Upon raising my head, I watched as two of the most beautiful, large powerful-looking beings descended down to either side of the head of the bed. I sat upright, and the recliner banged as it fell into the sitting position. I knew that I was fully awake, and I dared not blink for fear of missing something. These two powerfully strong angelic beings were moving with such fluidity as they slowly bent forward and descended into place. Their eyes were closed as they leaned forward, and before I could grasp what they were doing, they faded away. I looked around the room and saw everything was the same as it had been before. What had just happened? Was this a dream?

"God?" I said aloud. "God, help me. Why are they here? Why are they just getting here? Haven't they been here all along?"

I began to feel fear. Not the same fear that I had been battling, not a fear of these beings, but the fear of why? Why are they here? Why now? What's happening? Are we going to need them? As I started to question God, an overwhelming feeling of power and strength came upon me, and I lay back down in the chair. I remembered how they looked: powerful, strong, large. They held something, but I couldn't tell what it was. I couldn't take my eyes off of their countenance to look at what they held or why they leaned and before I knew it, they were gone. They were here to help, that much I knew. They were here to protect. "God, what do we need protection from?" I received no answer.

I became so quickly aware that I was exhausted; I pushed "play" on the tape deck, stretched my arm through the bed rail and held Bob's hand. As I closed my eyes, I said, "Thank you for coming," and fell asleep. I thanked God for sending heavenly reinforcements; I thanked them for the strength that I felt.

A week or so later Stan, Paula and I were in the waiting room of one of the ICU rooms that Bob had been moved to. I was crying and scared, trying to convince myself and the both of them that Bob was going to be okay. I explained to them that there were angels around Bob, that I had seen them. I told them that I knew they were there, I just didn't know what they were doing. I explained what had happened in his room that night and told them that these very large, powerful beings were leaning forward and I just couldn't understand what they were doing. As I was trying to figure it out, trying to describe them, Stan took over.

"They're not leaning Kim, they're kneeling, like this." He rose from the chair and knelt down in the middle of the waiting room. He knelt on one knee and leaned his upper body forward a bit and bowed his head.

I was shocked. He had seen them! He had seen them! They were really there! We began to cry as we looked at each other. Through his tears he asked, "Don't you still see them?"

I shook my head, and continued to cry in amazement. I was humbled.

He said, "They're still here. They're not kneeling anymore, though. They are fighting now."

I knew I had seen them, but I was so grateful that God had given me this confirmation. He truly had sent angels to guard us.

> *Psalm 91:9-11 "If you make the Most High your dwelling—even the Lord, who is my refuge—then no harm will befall you, no disaster will come near your tent. For he will command his angels concerning you to guard you…" (NIV Bible)*

20
Just a Bump in the Road

The morning after the angels, Bob seemed markedly worse. His speech was worse. He was incontinent of stool and urine. He kept looking at me like he was in there somewhere but lost. He was Bob inside this malfunctioning body, and I didn't know how to get to him. I felt like I was slowly losing him. I was watching him slowly leave me, and I couldn't do anything to stop it!

Paula called to check on us and to tell us that Hope had called her very early that morning. Hope told her, "Ignore what is going to happen today." Paula felt that she needed to convey this to me. I didn't know what to make of it.

The neurologist came in, and after asking Bob to answer his barrage of questions, he told us "I'm going to send him for another MRI. I'm just not convinced that Bob has had a stroke. The MRI's just don't look like a typical stroke presentation."

"What is it then?" I asked.

"I don't know yet." He looked less confused than concerned. I don't know why, but I trusted him.

"Okay, another scan then. What are you looking for?" The tests seemed useless.

"We're looking to see if the infarcted area has increased in size."

"And if it has, is that why he seems to be getting worse?" OUCH. I had just said out loud what I had been trying to avoid – the admission that Bob was getting worse.

"Yes. Sometimes an infarcted area grows after the initial incident. The tissue is still reacting to the cause of the infarct; tissue is still dying."

"Will he get better? I mean, is it possible that after it reaches the full infarct area, it will start to shrink?" There was still a spark of hope.

"We just have to wait and see." He said that a lot. I think that neurologists are a lot like weathermen. They wait to see what is happening and then report it. Always with the, "We'll have to wait and see." Waiting again.

However, in waiting, there was hope. In waiting, there was room for Bob to get better. He wasn't necessarily giving us bad news. I know that I could have construed it as bad news, but I chose not to. I chose to hold on to that slight ray of hope. In that waiting, there was also silence. Bob had stopped talking. I don't know the reason. Was it because that his speech was becoming more and more garbled? Was it because he had nothing to say? Was he as scared as I was? I didn't know. I didn't have a lot to say either. We just waited. And hoped. I don't remember praying a lot. I didn't know what to say to God.

Another MRI was ordered, and we waited for the transporter to come and take us to radiology. Somewhere between the ordering of the MRI and the transporter showing up, Bob's brother Steve arrived. I don't remember the order of the arrivals, only that while we waited in the hallway with Bob on the stretcher, we were joined by Stan, Steve, Hope and even Hope's estranged husband. We stood in the hall and waiting room all on pins and needles. It seemed that the wait took forever.

Bob lay on the stretcher and used a tissue to wipe his mouth. He seemed to be drooling now. This was new. Stan stood on the side of the stretcher to Bob's right side, and I was on his left.

Bob looked at me with the most confused eyes and said, "Paw nee me."

Stan leaned over Bob and said, "What Bob? Your knee?"

Steve approached the stretcher as well. Bob looked at me and pointed down toward the end of the stretcher. Again he said, "Paw nee me!" He was adamant about whatever it was that he was trying to say. He looked at me with the most determined look and said it again slower, "P-a-w n-e-e m-e!"

Stan, Steve, and I tried frantically to decipher what he was trying to say. Bob was as frustrated as we were. He repeated himself slower and slightly louder, "P-A-W N-E-E M-E!"

He looked at me as if to say, "Help me, Kim." The look in his eyes said so much.

"I'm frustrated. Why can't you understand me? Help me." All we got was another "Paw nee me." Finally I told him to stop trying.

"Are you in pain, Bob?" I asked.

He shook his head.

"Do you need anything?"

Another shake of the head.

"Then just wait; it's okay. We'll talk later. Just try and relax, okay?"

He laid his head back on the stretcher and sighed. He shook his head, "No" and looked away from me. Was he disgusted that I couldn't figure it out, or was he disgusted that he couldn't explain it?

Stan kept up, "Bob, is it your knee?" He grabbed Bob's knee. "Does it hurt? Does it itch?" He began to scratch Bob's leg.

So funny that Stan is known by all of us as such a non-compassionate person, yet he was so very compassionate during this time. He changed Bob's clothes, cleaned him from incontinence, and now scratched his itch. He jumped right in where he felt he was needed.

The wait in the hallway seemed to last forever. As I sat and waited for the technician to let us in, I watched Stan try to communicate with Bob, listened to Hope talk to Steve about how God had miraculously healed her of brain cancer, and stared at my husband who was mentally slipping away from me. Life had taken such a weird turn.

The drool was getting worse. Bob was having a hard time keeping up with it with his small hospital box of Kleenex. I took one away from him and wiped the corner of his mouth. I had to squeeze his cheeks to try to expel the drool that he had obviously pocketed into them. Where was it all coming from? I spied a crash cart out of the corner of my eye and saw the suction canister on the back of it.

"Excuse me!" I heard myself call out to the radiology technician, "Can you hook up that suction canister and get me a yankur tip for him? He's got a lot of secretions that he doesn't seem to be able to clear."

"Sure, hold on." She busied herself trying to find the proper connections and suction catheter.

I don't know how, but the nurse in me surfaced again. I don't know where she came from. I was in such a funk sitting by his side listening to him garble every word, so tired of cleaning him of his incontinence every few hours, so scared of what was happening and wondering if I'd ever have my husband back again, and then snap! The next thing I knew I was standing in the hallway telling a technician to hook up the portable suction canister to a yankur suction tip and stretching the tubes across the hallway to clear Bob's secretions from his mouth.

"Spit, Bob, spit!" I'd say. He tried. I handed him the hard plastic suction wand and told him to use it himself. "When you feel all of those secretions, that drool in your mouth, just suck it out with this if you can't spit, okay?"

I didn't know why he had so much drool or where it was coming from.

The technician finally came out, and said, "We're ready for Bob now."

Hope stood up from the waiting room, "Kim, I'd like to go in with him if you don't mind. I want to pray for him while he's having this MRI."

I didn't mind at all. I was silently thankful that one of the warriors was going to be with him, and it wouldn't have to be me. It was so hard to watch him like this. I watched the technician push his stretcher into the scan room and watched Hope follow closely behind. I walked into the waiting room and sat in the chair. The waiting room looked different than it had the first few times. Why? I don't know.

I was so tired.

I laid my head back against the wall and closed my eyes. What seemed like two seconds later, Bob's stretcher was back in the hall.

"We'll call for the transporter to take him back. It shouldn't be long." Every time we waited for a transporter, it was long. The tests were short, the waiting was long.

Savannah showed up. Same broom handle legs, same sweet smile. Stan and I looked at each other and smiled. It was nice to have some consistency. Stan helped push this time.

We arrived back in the room, and I asked the nurses to hook up the suction at his bedside.

"Okay, let's get some vital signs, too." They took Bob's vitals, all okay. We were all so tired. Stan went to the waiting room and fell asleep on the couch. Hope stayed with me.

I can remember lying Bob on his side so that the drool would roll out of his mouth and onto the pillow. I put a towel on the pillow under his cheek. I watched the towel fill with drool. Where was it coming from? At least he looked peaceful. He looked like he was sleeping. Dare I try to get some rest?

Steve's wife Susan arrived shortly after Bob fell asleep. She was asking a lot of questions, questions for which neither I nor the doctors had answers. She didn't seem satisfied with the fact that I didn't know what was happening. Neither was I, but what were we to do but wait and see what the damage from the apparent stroke was?

I don't know when I realized that Bob's breathing was becoming more labored and the secretions seemed to be increasing. Was it when the nurses came in to get his vital signs again? Was it when they came to give him his medication? They sat Bob up and handed him the medicine cup with two pills in it.

"Here's your aspirin and seizure pill, Bob." The nurse handed him a cup of water to swallow the pills with. Bob took the medicine cup and looked at me. He had the most confused look on his face.

"Those are your pills, Bob. Go ahead and take them." Why did he look to me for everything? He tipped the cup up to his mouth and began to chew the pills.

"Bob, no! Swallow, Bob, swallow!" I handed him the water cup. "Wash it down, Bob!"

The nurse and I looked at each other. I felt like screaming. "Someone help us. He's getting worse! When will this end?!" It wouldn't end any time soon, and no one had any answers. She knew that he was getting worse, too. She had no answers either.

I sat beside his bed and watched the rise and fall of his chest. I sat beside him and wiped the drool from his chin. I was too tired to cry, too exhausted to think. When had I slept last? Had I eaten that day?

The nurse took Bob's vital signs again and told me that he had a fever, 102.5. What I didn't know until later was that Bob's blood counts from that morning showed that his white blood count was down to practically zero. The chemo had done its job. Bob's white blood cells were nadiring, and now he had developed an infection somewhere. He would soon be septic.

Before I knew it, the room filled with nurses. They placed the probe on his finger to detect the level of oxygen in his blood. It was in the 80's. Way too low. Bob needed help breathing; he needed to be intubated fast.

The nurse and I looked over the bed at each other, and I told her, "Please get someone to help him. He needs help!"

She left at a run, and within minutes, the room was full of doctors and nurses. Tim, Joey, and Jeff were there first.

We sat Bob up in bed. "Breathe, Bob, deep breath!" I ordered him to breathe. "Bob, look at me! Look at me, Bob!" He was becoming more and more confused, less and less responsive. Oh, God, help! "Bob! You have to breathe! Listen to me, Bob. Deep breath." I suctioned his mouth and continued to yell at him to breathe. Oh, God, help! We were losing him. He could hardly sit up on his own. The doctors were holding him up and listening to his lungs with their stethoscopes, staring at the pulse oximeter that was reading lower and lower. As if they didn't know what was happening, as if they were only waiting for my permission, as if they were still weighing their options, I offered my frantic opinion to them.

"He needs help breathing; he needs to go on a breathing machine."

The resident stared at me. "We'll be right back."

They were back, in what seemed like seconds, all three of them and one other doctor.

She was short with a full face, strawberry blonde hair and an air of authority around her that told me that she was the one to talk to. "Hi, I'm Dr. Peterson, and I'm here to help. Is this your husband?"

"Yes. He needs help breathing, NOW!" We had waited long enough. I didn't care about introductions. I couldn't keep suctioning him. I couldn't keep yelling at him to breathe. He needed to go on the breathing machine. Now.

She was so calm, "Yes. We're going to help him breathe now. We're going to stick a tube down his throat and breathe for him for awhile."

As she was speaking in that calm voice, a flurry of activity went on around her. The nurses were running into the room with the crash cart, the respiratory therapy team had arrived and were pulling his bed out into the middle of the room.

Someone laid Bob back on the bed and began to pull the headboard of the bed off. Oh, dear God, it was really happening. Bob was being emergently intubated.

As Dr. Peterson stood in the corner of the room being gowned and gloved by a nurse, she looked over her shoulder and spoke again in that calming voice, "Kim, do you want to stay in the room?"

"No!" I couldn't. I had seen too many codes, had witnessed too many patients being treated like... patients. Not Bob. I wouldn't watch him go through that. He was still my Bob, my husband. I didn't want that memory. I didn't want to have to go to sleep at night seeing my husband being intubated in my dreams. The room was so full of people, strangers. Where was Bob's nurse, someone who knew him?

I leaned over Bob's chest, put my face up to his and said, "Bob, the doctors are going to help you now. They're going to put a tube in your throat to help you breathe. It won't be for long, and I'll be right here when you wake up. Do you hear me, Bob?" He nodded his head. He made eye contact with me and shook his head. "I love you, Bob. Just close your eyes and think of Jesus, okay? Pray, Bob, pray!" I kissed him on the forehead and told him, "It'll be okay."

He lifted his left hand and gave me the thumbs up sign. Then he said the first comprehensible sentence that he'd said in twenty-four hours and the last words that he would say for three months, "Just a bump in the road." It gave me such hope. I repeated that sentence over and over for three months.

I pulled myself away from him with that image. It was a good one to hold on to.

As I walked past Dr. Peterson, I asked her, "Will you be doing this?"

"Yes." She nodded her head and smiled.

I touched her shoulder and prayed for her, "Please, God, let her do a good job."

"It'll be over in just a few minutes; I'll be right out to get you."

I walked numbly out to the waiting room. Stan and Hope were walking away from me. Steve, Susan, and Dave were there. Mom and Dad were just coming up the hall. Mom started running and crying because she had seen the crash cart being wheeled into Bob's room.

Someone said to her, "It's okay; they're just intubating him." Why was that okay? Why was that supposed to sound comforting? They're just intubating him. No big deal. Don't let the crash cart and twenty-five people inside Bob's room scare you; they're just emergently putting him on a breathing machine.

Remember how Hope had told Paula to ignore what was going to happen today? It was hard to ignore this one.

* * * * * * *

I walked into the waiting room and sat on the edge of the couch so briefly that you would have thought that there were needles on it. I jumped up and started to pace. The waiting room was too small, too many chairs and too many people. Why was the TV on? Who was watching TV? I went outside the waiting room to pace back and forth in the hall. I noticed that I was praying out loud, in tongues. I had received the gift of speaking in tongues many years earlier. This gift is described in the Bible in the Book of Acts. Suffice it to say that in time of need, when you can't find the words to say, the Holy Spirit intercedes for us through this gift. Once I realized that I was praying out loud, I noticed that others were watching me. I didn't care at the time. What were they thinking? I still don't care. I needed God in a big way, and all I could do to get myself through was to pray. There were no words, so God provided them.

As I paced, my dad walked behind me. Step for step. I turned, he turned. I stopped, he stopped. Was he following me for fear that I might fall? Would he be able to pick me up if I did?

Why was this taking so long? Steve started asking my mom and dad if he should call his parents. My parents told him to get them on the phone immediately. Dave was worried that he hadn't told his parents to come back sooner. I remember listening to Dave, Steve, and Susan try and decide whether or not they should tell Bob's parents to drive or fly. I remember watching them huddled together in the waiting room trying to figure out what to tell the parents. I remember hearing my dad say with the tone of authority that I'd heard all my life, "You tell your parents to go to the airport right now and get on the next plane to Denver!"

Oh, dear God, this was serious. Why was it taking so long to sink in? None of us wanted to admit that Bob was so serious. It was okay, they were just intubating him. One of the nurses came out to see us.

"Dr. Peterson is the best. Bob is okay. The procedure went well."

Dr. Peterson came out shortly thereafter. Still calm. Smiling a very respectful smile. "Everything went well. The respiratory therapists are getting him ready to travel to the unit. We'll put him in the BMT unit and put him on a ventilator. I'll keep a close eye on him."

"Thank you." It is hard to thank one who has just intubated your husband, but what else do you say? "Can I go see him?"

I walked in the room, and Bob was lying there on that same bed that had been pulled out to the middle of the room with the headboard still off. The bright procedure lights were shining down on him. The room was a mess. Apparently, no one was concerned with hitting a trash can while emergently intubating a patient.

Bob lay there in a drug-induced stupor, his hands tied to the bed rails. I reached out and grabbed his wrists above where the restraints were and looked up at the woman standing there taping the tube into his mouth.

"He tried to pull the tube out; it's very common, so we do that to protect him." I knew, but I still hated seeing him that way.

I leaned over and kissed his forehead again. "It's over, Bob. You're going to be fine. They'll just help you breathe for a while. Just rest. Let them do the work for a while. You just rest and get better." I talked for myself. I knew that he didn't hear me.

"Kim," my mom called from the doorway, "There's a doctor out here who wants to talk to us."

Dr. Carlton was one of Dr. Jeffries' colleagues from the Bone Marrow Transplant offices. He was a short man with glasses, very serious-looking. "Hi, I'm Dr. Carlton, here for Dr. Jeffries who is out of town. How are you doing?" he asked in a very serious tone.

Oh, just fine. How was I doing? Why do doctors ask these pleasant little questions? Do they really want an answer? I don't remember giving him an answer. I do remember looking around. Stan was back. Bob's brothers were a mess. Dave was crying, and so was my dad. I felt like I was in a dream, and he was talking to wake me up.

"Mrs. Hritz, Bob is a 9 ½ out of 10 on the critically ill scale." He paused to let that sink in. "We're doing everything we can for him, but we don't know if he'll make it through the night."

My dream was turning into a nightmare, and I wasn't waking. "Well, you don't know my husband! He's a 10 out of 10 on the toughness scale, and he's going to be fine."

Not only did he not know my husband, he didn't know me. I wasn't giving up that easily. "We believe in God, and we're praying," I told him. It sounded so simple, meant so much. We believe. There is so much power in belief, so much power in faith. Faith as small as a mustard seed can move mountains. We were going to move a mountain.

He tried to convince me of how serious the situation was, like I needed to be convinced! I suppose that not knowing me, he could have thought that I was in denial. He could have thought that I was naïve to what was happening. I was not in denial. I was fully aware, and I was not naïve to the enemy's plan. He had just delivered what he thought to be a life-threatening blow. Though exhausted beyond comprehension, I was in no way backing down now. This fight wasn't over by a long shot. I knew that God still had a few miracles up His sleeve, and I was going to stand and wait for mine! And I was MAD! How dare Satan think that he could take my husband away from me!

Dr. Carlton explained that they were concerned that Bob had suffered from a pulmonary embolism, a blood clot in his lung, which would explain why he had stopped breathing.

My gut told me that wasn't the case. I shook my head, "I don't think it's a P.E." I spoke to him as if he were asking my medical opinion.

He explained that it would be the logical assumption. They were assuming again, making a weatherman diagnosis again.

Dr. Carlton stated that Bob would need to go down to Interventional Radiology to have a Greenfield filter placed in his aortic vein. This filter would stop any further clots from traveling to his brain or lungs. It would be the prudent thing to do in this situation. Even if they were not sure if Bob were throwing clots, it would be good preventative medicine.

"It's not a clot…" I said softly, but since he wasn't listening to me, I turned and told my mother, "It's not a clot." Why was I so sure?

She explained that the filter would not be detrimental to Bob. That was the best argument I heard and agreed.

Dr. Carlton saw that my mom had convinced me and stated, "You will need to go with him to sign the consent forms. You can take one other person with you." Thank God my mom was there!

Then Dr. Carlton said one more thing to us, to Bob's family and to my family that let us know how serious he had been. "I'll have the nurses call someone from pastoral care to come and speak with you all. If you need to call any other family members, now would be the time."

"We don't need her!" Stan jumped in, remembering the earlier visit from the pastoral care worker. They seemed to want to talk more of grieving and accepting death than believing for life.

Bob's family didn't understand that we'd already had our fill of the pastoral care department. "Thanks for speaking for all of us," I heard one of them say in a rather hurt tone.

Stan replied, "We met her; we don't need her right now. Bob will be fine." We were still believing. He sounded so sure.

My mother and I followed the bed that the nurses were pushing downstairs. Dr. Carlton stayed with us. The respiratory technician was breathing for Bob by squeezing bag that was connected to the tube that had been placed down

Bob's throat. He was in a drug-induced sleep and looked so peaceful. After we arrived at the radiology department, my mom and I were ushered into a small room with a table and a few chairs. The chairs were ridiculously short and reminded me of ones that one would see in a kindergarten class. I sat in one of those chairs and rested my hands on my knees that were unnaturally close to my chin.

Before I could figure out why this room was furnished for five-year-olds, another doctor, wearing scrubs, came in. He looked genuinely concerned about Bob. He explained the procedure for placing the filter and suggested that at the same time we place a central I.V. line. I signed the consent forms and nodded my head. "Yes, yes, I understand," I said but at the same time, no, no, I didn't.

I was so afraid, so numb that I had to concentrate on keeping it together. I quietly talked to myself, "Kim, calm down. It is going to be fine. Breathe." My heart was beating so fast it was hard to control my breathing. "Breathe." Was this what a panic attack felt like? "Breathe." The room was too small to pace in, so I continued to talk to myself.

The procedure was over quickly, and this time there was no waiting for a transporter. Dr. Carlton and the respiratory technician were there to take us back upstairs to the BMT unit. They told us that they would stay with him until he settled in, which apparently meant until he was connected to the ventilator that was being delivered to his room.

My mom and I walked back to the elevator with Dr. Carlton. I walked through the basement radiology department of the hospital, following the bed with a respiratory technician bagging life into my husband with each new squeeze of the ambulatory bag. I tried to control my breathing to coincide with the breaths that Bob was receiving. I couldn't breathe that slowly. My heart was still beating too fast. "Calm down...breathe," I kept telling myself.

The elevator doors opened, and they pushed Bob out and to the right. They pointed us to the left and told us to wait in the waiting room until they settled Bob into his new room. It didn't feel like we were gone that long, but there were people in the waiting room waiting for us.

Family members were there. I don't remember who was there; I just remember realizing that there were more people than before. I immediately realized that I needed to see Aimie and Katie. "I need the girls! I have to call them."

My mom told me that someone had already called Paula, and she was bringing Katie. I had to call Aimie at school and tell her that Bob was in the ICU. I left a message on her cell phone and told her to please come home...now.

I hated that I had to leave it, but she hadn't returned any of my calls over the past few days. I was running out of patience and possibly time. The message was short and anything but sweet. "Aimie, Bob is in the ICU at the hospital. He stopped breathing, and he's on life support. I need you, now."

The first time I saw him after he was "settled," I walked in to the room as if I were walking into a dream. I don't remember if I were alone, I don't remember if the nurse came and got me, or if I went in to ask if I could go in. I do remember that he was in the room directly next to the nurse's station. Later I found out that was the room reserved for their most critical patients.

The nurses directed me to him. They were unbelievably awesome. If I were to write a book about how wonderful they were, I couldn't describe it. God blessed us with them, every day. They made the move to the ICU less traumatic and somewhat comforting. They let me know that they would take care of him now. I trusted them.

21
Please Leave the Radio On

I entered his room. Forget the dream; this was a nightmare. He was lying there in bed, ventilator at his bedside breathing for him, tubes taped to his face. Three I.V. pumps were next to the head of his bed full of various sized bags of fluid. A bag of blood was dripping into the newly-placed central line. His wrists were still tied to the bed rails. There was a foley catheter bag hanging from the bed. Evidently, these were all things he had acquired in the "settling" process.

He was as pale as the bed sheets and as still as death. The room seemed huge and was quiet except for the rhythm of machine noises. Though he was still holding an additional fifteen pounds from the steroids, he seemed so small in it. There were hospital things everywhere. It was so clinical. He seemed so lost in it all. It didn't seem like Bob; it was all so unreal.

I walked across the room to his bedside, and I spoke to him as if he were listening. "Bob, I know you're in there. I'll be waiting for you. Take all the time you need, but come back to me, Bob. I'm not leaving you. Don't leave me." I didn't cry. I was numb. I laid my head on his chest and prayed. "God, hold him now, but let him come back." I had nothing else to say.

I didn't stay long in his room. I didn't know where to go. I went back and forth from the waiting room to his room so many times that first night. The nurses were so accommodating. Did they think it was going to be my last few hours with my husband? They let me come and go as I pleased. Visiting hours meant nothing.

Bob's parents showed up, and the waiting room began to fill up with others as well. His sisters from Alabama and Ohio were there, John from work came, Katie and Paula were there, my parents and my brother Stan were still there. People were everywhere.

Every time someone new came in the waiting room, I would tell him/her, "I'll take you in to see him." The speech that I gave was always the same, "He looks bad, and there are a lot of tubes and I.V. lines, but don't get worried. He's comfortable and will be okay, he's just resting, and the breathing machine is just going to help him breathe for awhile. Don't be upset when you see him, and don't say anything upsetting. Just talk to him like normal. Just speak to him like he's awake and listening."

I didn't want us to bring in our fear and worry. I wanted him to hear us speaking life. If he thought we were okay, he'd not worry about us. Each person went in and stopped in the doorway. The sight was overwhelming. The room was dimly lit and quiet except for the machine whirring and occasional sound of air being forced into his body. It was eerie. I would let the new visitor get accustomed to the sight and walk him/her closer to his bed. Every time I walked someone new up to his bed, it was like a spouse walking loved ones up to a casket at a wake. "Doesn't he look good?"

"Yes, he looks peaceful." What else do you say? The first night we didn't know what to say.

One of my trips to his room that first night I noticed that there was a radio on the table in his room. I immediately found the Christian radio station and turned it on low. Praise and worship music was a must. I told the nurses, "Please don't turn the radio off. This station plays praise and worship music, and the Bible says that God inhabits the praises of His people, so if there is praise and worship music here, God will inhabit this room. We need Him here."

I told them every night before I left. I also told them, "I will be listening to the same station at home next to my bed, and I want to know that he's hearing the same thing that I'm hearing every night." They obliged. One of them even wrote a note and stuck it to the radio, "PER KIM: PLEASE LEAVE RADIO ON, AND DON'T CHANGE THE STATION." We were welcoming God in with praise and worship music.

Psalm 100:4 Enter his gates with thanksgiving and his courts with praise…(NIV Bible)

When Katie arrived, she would not go into the room with me. "No, I'm not going to see him like this, and you can't make me go in!" I was okay with that, as long as she stayed in the waiting room with me. Aimie eventually received the message and came. She and her friend Debbie walked into the waiting room, and Aimie walked straight past, almost through me.

"Where is he!?" She'd been crying and her face was red and her eyes puffy. I stood to hug her, but she was not going to be stopped and continued to walk toward the ICU doors. I told her that I'd take her to him. When Aimie arrived, Katie stood up and followed her toward the doors with as much determination as Aimie had walked in with. She was coming with us.

I took them into the room, and they hesitated upon entering, both of them catching their breath and immediately breaking down into tears. They stood in the doorway and hugged each other, crying.

"God, this is too hard to watch," I spoke softly. I made them come close to him; I made them talk to him. I made them touch him. I told them that he could hear us. I told them to talk to him just like he was listening. They did. They were awesome. Aimie talked, joked, and scolded him for being sick. Katie was more reserved. She didn't want to talk to him yet. She was petrified.

We stood next to him and listened to the radio. I told them that we should just pray and believe God, and that Bob was in no pain right now. A song came on the radio, and Aimie and I sang to him. Through tears and sobs, off-key we sang. Good thing Bob couldn't hear.

The girls were so strong and so full of faith. They prayed with me and laid hands on Bob as they prayed for his healing. They adjusted quickly to Bob's near death look and decided to not stand for it. "We're not going to put up with this crap, Bob! Now knock it off and get better!" Aimie would say. "Hey, let's paint his toenails hot pink and shave off one of his eye brows!"

"Bob, you'd better get up and protect yourself," I would laugh with them. I guess it made us feel better to laugh at the situation. What else could we do?

After ushering everyone in to see him, and telling them that he was safe because nothing could happen to him now, I went home. Paula says she drove me home, and she slept with me. I don't remember. I don't remember anything about that night except that I knew that Bob's condition had worsened to a point that I couldn't even fathom was possible. Maybe our minds protect us by not remembering things like this. Try as I might, and I have tried, I have asked everyone who was there about what happened that night. Where did I go? What did I do? Did I leave the hospital? Did I go home? I still don't remember.

22
Cleft in the Rock

I lost any sense of control that night. For the first three days of this hospitalization, I didn't want to leave his side, but when Bob was put on life support and taken to the ICU, I started to lose my grip on being his caretaker. I realized that he was going to need more than I could give. It was out of my hands. It was completely out of my hands.

I prayed, "God, hold him. Keep him. Fix this." I was numb, completely numb. I was being removed from the situation; God was moving me. I could feel it: He was moving me to a new place. It was a comforting feeling to be so out of control. It was such a weird thing for me, control-freak me, to be comforted in losing control. This had to be God. I knew it was Him.

The doctors still couldn't tell us what was wrong. They were conferring every day and still not coming up with any answers. The consensus was that the area of infarction in his brain was causing him to have seizures, and the area seemed to be growing. We sat by helplessly and watched Bob deteriorate as we waited for the area to stop getting worse. It kept getting worse, however.

They knew for sure that there was some brain damage. Was it a stroke? Why were the MRI's showing that the area of infarction was changing? Was it not a stroke? Why was he getting worse? It seemed like we relied so heavily on the labs, the x-rays, the MRI's, but the doctors were guessing. I knew it. They, like Stan, were trying to gather as much information, as many puzzle pieces as they could. They still didn't know because nothing fit. I could tell by the answers to our questions, their body language, and their apologies every time they walked into the waiting room.

As a result, I stopped asking questions that I knew they had no answers for. I just stated the obvious, "We'll just have to wait and see, right?"

They always answered with a sad nod of the head, "Can I do anything for you, Kim?"

"Take care of him the best you can." That was all I could say. Occasionally, I would ask one of the doctors "Do you pray? Will you pray for him and just do the best you can?" A few told me that they would and that they had already started praying for him.

I knew that Bob was going to be safe now – no more telling him to breathe, no more suctioning the drool from his mouth. They were taking care of him now, and God had him. They were watching him as closely as I had, and he was safe with God. There was nothing I could do now. I couldn't even pray at first.

I was back to "God?! What's going on?!" I couldn't even articulate a prayer. "God, please help! Please help!"

I cried every time I prayed, and I was trying so hard not to cry that I stopped praying. I just waited on God to move. I knew He was there, knew that He was aware of what we were going through, knew that I would have to wait not only on Bob's condition to change, but also wait on the doctors to give us some information. I also knew I had to wait on God. As long as I knew that God was working, I could wait. How long though, God?

The doctors wanted me to sign more consents for more tests. "Do whatever you need to," I told them. I had tried so long to sit by him, to fix him, to hold on; now I was letting go. God was allowing me to let go, not of Bob, but of control. I wasn't letting go of my hope, I was just letting go of my sense of control. I never really had it, so I guess I just lost my illusion of control.

    That evening when they took Bob away from me and put him in the BMT ICU, when they stuck a tube down his throat and began to breathe for him, when they pumped his body full of I.V. drugs and blood cells, he was no longer mine to protect. The void that was created was immediately being filled by God. He became so strong to me. He became so real. He became so big while I became so small. I was laying Bob down to God. I was giving him over to God. I was laying my sacrifice at God's altar. I would have to lay it down. I would have to let it go.

* * * * * * *

    Bob's white blood count was still very low due to the effects of the high-dose chemotherapy. His red blood count dropped low enough that he received two units of packed red blood cells. He was on a ventilator with tubes down his throat. He had a central line in his chest with four lumens, each of them plugged with an I.V. line of some sort, and he had a foley catheter and eventually a rectal tube. He had an arterial line in his left wrist that connected to a monitor that read his central venous pressures. He was hooked up to an EKG monitor so that we could watch every heart beat. He was wired and tubed everywhere. I wasn't afraid that he would die; how could he? He had a machine to do his breathing, his heart was fine, and the IV fluids were keeping him hydrated. I rationalized that this was okay, he was safe now. He didn't have to fight anymore. He was resting, and the medical team was helping him to stay alive now.

Joey, Tim and Jeff came into the room one day. Jeff said, "We'd like to do a lumbar puncture to see if his cerebral spinal fluid is clear."

I knew that I should just let them do whatever they wanted at this point. I remember thinking the day before when the medical student had said something about a lumbar puncture, "His white blood count is next to nothing, and you want to poke a needle into his spine??" It didn't make sense. Maybe I was still, at that point, hoping that he'd just get better, and we'd go home. Now I didn't care what they did as long as they fixed him.

I remember when I was in labor delivering Aimie, the doctor asked if a student could observe. I was in active labor and honestly didn't care if the doctor brought a marching band into the room; I just wanted that baby out of me. This feeling was similar. I'll sign anything; I just want my husband back. It was in their hands now. Don't bother me with the details…fix him!!

I signed consents for the lumbar puncture, I signed consents for blood transfusions, I signed another consent (I know there were three); I just don't remember what the third was for. Wow, it was so unlike me. I was giving up, giving in. Take him. I'm letting go.

I can remember someone in the waiting room asking "Do you think a lumbar puncture is necessary?" Bob's family was there with me. They had many questions. They hadn't let go yet. They still believed that they were somehow in control. "What are you looking for? Why are you still testing him? What about the risk of infection?" All good questions, but I had already signed the consents. I had already given them permission, had already lost control. It took them longer to lose control.

Once I stopped trying to be Bob's doctor, stopped trying to control everything about his medical care, stopped trying to fix it all myself, I changed. I allowed myself to fall into a weird void of nothingness.

I kept asking God, "What's happening? Why?"

All I heard was, "Shhhh. It's okay." Literally, I heard "Shhhhh," then felt the "It's okay."

I knew that God was hiding me. He was behind me, to the left of me, to the right of me, and the only opening was in front of me. However, He had His hand in front of me, holding me back.

I explained it to anyone who would listen like this, "Remember when God put Moses in the cleft in the rock? That's where I am."

I was in the cleft. I was so safe. There was so much strength surrounding me. It was going to be okay. I didn't have to figure it out, didn't have to fix anything. Just shhhh, just shut up and wait. Naturally, it was so hard for me, but I did it. I shut up, and I waited.

Bob was sick, possibly going to die, even that night. I was vividly aware that God was moving me from a place of feeling like I had control, to a place of quiet peace. I didn't know why, but I knew that Bob was in a new safe place, and I was being placed somewhere safe, too.

I can remember telling Bob's sisters, Kathy and Mary, in the waiting room that I felt like I was in that cleft in the rock. "I'm okay. It's like God has put me in a place, in a crack in a rock. There's no where else to go. It's like a big rock—behind me is rock, on both sides of me is rock. It's a very safe feeling. The only opening is in the front, and God has His hand over it, blocking me from getting out. All God will say to me is, 'Shhhh. It's okay.'"

That was enough. I told anyone who would listen. I was safe. It was okay. I heard myself saying this over and over. Some people looked at me so sadly. I could see it in their eyes, could read what they were thinking, "You poor thing, I'm so sorry."

I wondered why they looked at me like that. Why were they sorry for me? I was okay; God had just told me. I was in a safe place.

All sense of time left while I was in that rock. All sense of anyone else left. I knew only God. I felt only God. I was so close to Him. At times I long for that feeling again, but doubt that I could stand what it might take to get there.

I don't know when I ate, or if I ate. I don't remember the first four days in any chronological sense of time. I only remember a few details, and I only remember that I was in a safe place, very safe place. So was Bob. Bob was only in the BMT ICU for four days. Those first four days seemed like forever. I can't believe it was only four days?! Seriously, only four days? These were the longest four days of my existence.

Some people looked at me, and I could tell that they knew where I was. Some didn't. I could tell by the look in people's eyes whether or not they saw where I was. Some thought that I needed their help, but they didn't know the help that was needed. I began to feel sorry for people who were trying to help me. I didn't know what they thought they could do. It was all in God's hands now. I knew I needed help, but I knew where to find it. I also knew that I was desperate for the help that only God could provide. And He provided. I wished that He would provide that safe place, that place of help for everyone. Unfortunately, not everyone was open to His help.

There were times when people would pull me from that place of safety. They would speak to me, and try to comfort me with empty words, empty actions, or with food. I remember watching others planning meals and thinking, "How can they eat? How can they leave?" There was such a production involved in the planning. I couldn't understand it.

I don't remember any meals; I only remember drinking coffee. Stan brought me coffee, a lot. It was warm and sweet and comforting and probably the only thing that kept me walking.

A wonderful and dear woman from our church owned a deli and heard that my family and I were practically living at the hospital, so they brought sandwiches, soup, and cannolis to us frequently. She brought boxes of food. I watched as my family and Bob's dug through the boxes and handed out sandwiches and cookies.

"Kim, you have to eat. When is the last time you ate?"

I didn't remember, I didn't care.

I remember Stan going to get coffee and asking me if I wanted some. "I'm going to get you some coffee. When did you eat last?" He came back and brought me two cups. "I didn't know what kind you wanted, regular or French vanilla, so I brought both." Smart. He sat them on the table in our new living room. I drank them both. The French vanilla was so sweet; why had I not realized how cold I was until I picked up that warm coffee? It was so comforting. I drank it in and enjoyed the sweetness of the coffee and the sweetness of God's presence. Why was everyone so worried about food, and why was everyone so worried about my eating?

What I realized later was that I hadn't eaten and that my family was worried because they were afraid I would make myself sick. I began to lose weight, my face looked sunken, and my eyes looked hollow. Eventually, they began to force me to eat. I resented feeling like I was being forced to feed my flesh when I was tying to ignore my flesh. The cleft in the rock was such a place of spiritual awareness. I wanted to be more spiritually aware and closer to God and ignore the natural. There was nothing happening in the natural that I wanted to be a part of anyway. However, I couldn't let myself get sick, because I had to stay healthy and strong for Bob. I had to be there for him. Slowly I came back to the world of the natural. As much as I hated to be there, I had to.

As we sat in the waiting room day by day, I watched people coming and going. I listened to everyone talking and trying to figure out what was wrong with Bob and how they could fix him. I felt so alone in that waiting room full of people. I missed Bob so much. I just wanted to talk to him, just for a minute. I remember imagining that he was there, imagining him listening to me. What would he say? What would his advice be?

When I spoke to Rusty on the phone, he kept telling me, "Bob would tell you to stop worrying; he'd tell you to be strong." It helped, but I wanted to hear Bob's voice. I wanted to hear him. I missed hearing his voice.

I'd been away from Bob before. He had gone on fishing trips with his friends. Those trips were always hard in the beginning of our relationship. Later in our marriage, I began to accept his trips. I knew he was coming back, knew he was having fun and de-stressing. We talked every day, and I had faith he'd be back. This time I was working very hard at having faith that he'd be back. Aimie told me that she had been calling Bob's cell phone just to hear his voice on the answering machine. That made me so sad. I decided to try it myself. I kept his phone with me and listened to it often. I wondered if I'd ever hear him speak again.

23
Should I Stay or Should I Go?

The waiting room to the BMT unit became our home. We laughed at the fact that we called half of it our living room and the other half our den. The "living room" had two couches, a coffee table, an end table, a round table with two chairs, and a television. There was another chair and end table with a phone. The phone never worked, but it didn't matter because there was no one to call. The "den" consisted of a round table and four comfortable low chairs. They sat next to a large window with a view of the roof of part of the hospital. The best part of the den window is that it provided a glimpse of the sky, so that we could see that patch of blue.

Our new living room and den were book-ended by two sets of doors. One door led to the bone marrow transplant unit. One set of double electric doors led to the rest of the hospital. It was a closed-off part of the third floor of the hospital, and there was not a lot of traffic, only those who were going to the unit. It was somewhat private as far as hospital waiting rooms are concerned. We spent the most part of the next two months in those rooms. We took over. If Bob were going to live there, so were we.

The first four days, there were enough visitors that we filled the living room and den. Bob's family and my family we were all sitting there every day… waiting… waiting… waiting.

I would go into Bob's room and sit in a chair at the end of his bed and stare at him. I would lay my head on his chest and feel the machine give him rhythmic breaths. I would pace my breathing with his. I would talk to him and continually tell him, "I know you're in there. I know that God has you. I know you're safe. Take your time and get what you need wherever you are, but come back to me, Bob. When you're ready, come back to me. I'll wait. I'll be here. I'm not leaving you; please don't leave me."

There were nights I remember that I couldn't leave. I didn't know if I should stay with him all night or go home. I couldn't make up my mind. I was so tired, so exhausted, but so scared to leave. What if something happened while I was gone? I felt like my being there was the only thing keeping him alive.

Nights were hard. I was physically, mentally, and emotionally drained. I would argue with myself, "Should I stay all night here with him? Should I go home and sleep in my bed?"

It was such a difficult decision every single night. I fought the same fear every night. What if I leave him, and he dies while I'm gone? One night in particular I remember having the "Go-or-Stay" argument. Paula and Stan were there, and so was Mary. Everyone just wanted to appease me. They stood and watched me argue with myself.

"I'm staying," I would say confidently as I pulled out the sleeper bed and plopped myself upon it. Then I would cry, "Should I go home? I can't sleep here; this is so uncomfortable. Who will be with Katie? I should go home, shouldn't I?"

They all looked at me, "Whatever you want, Kim."

"I can't leave him though, what if something happens?"

I would cry again. The argument went on longer than usual, and the lack of food and sleep had evidently gotten to me. I was completely a mess. I watched them all watch me and hated them for being so wishy-washy. Why couldn't someone just tell me what to do?

Paula finally stood up to me and put an end to the indecision, "Make up your mind! You are staying or going, but we're not going to sit here and watch you cry about it all night!"

Wow.

"You're acting like a tired two-year-old. You need some sleep, now decide."

"Alright! I'm going home, but I can't sleep alone. Someone has to sleep with me." I did sound like a two-year-old. I felt guilty for leaving him, but I couldn't stay. I lay myself across his torso and cried.

"Bob, I have to go home and sleep. I can't stay; I'm tired; I can't do this."

I don't know how long I lay there; I felt someone pulling me away from the bed. I hooked my hand under the far bed rail. I was going to fight to stay now that I'd made up my mind to leave? It was so confusing.

Someone pried my fingers away; I think Paula took a tone of authority again. The next thing I remember, I was in the back seat of my car, laying across the seat and crying like that spoiled two-year-old again, really crying this time. I was sobbing and was having a hard time catching my breath. Paula yelled from the front seat for me to shut up. Mary was driving my car and commented on the way it cornered. I was trying to stop crying and breathe.

"Turn up the radio; this is a good song!" I managed between sobs.

They did, and we all listened to the same song that was playing in Bob's room. I don't remember the song, but I do remember that it stopped me from crying.

All forty-three nights that Bob stayed in the hospital, I had that same argument over whether to go home or to stay the night. It was never quite as bad as that night, but it was always there.

The pastoral care woman came back sometime early on in Bob's stay. She wanted to prepare handouts for our family to help us to grieve. Here it was, grieving again. I refused to take the paperwork. She packaged the grieving paperwork up and handed me the packages: one for me, one for Aimie, and one for Katie. I laid them on the table and walked away from them. Katie and Paula and I sat in the waiting room one night and looked through the pamphlets that were on the wall. We laughed at some of them. "Is Johnny Fighting at School: How Teenagers Handle Grief." Paula asked Katie, "Are you fighting at school, Katie?" We all laughed. We laughed at such inappropriate times and at such weird things.

* * * * * * *

The Bible taught me that faith is seeing what you believe and not what you actually see. While we continued to "call things that weren't as though they were" and state repeatedly that Bob was fine, his physical condition continued to worsen. My physical condition worsened, work worsened (though I didn't care), and my relationship with anyone else around me became unimportant.

The doctors had finally diagnosed Bob. He was suffering from encephalitis. They believed that the steroids had weakened his immune system, and the first dose of chemotherapy pushed his immune system even deeper into compromise. In that state of severely compromised immune system, he had developed sepsis and encephalitis. The lumbar puncture had shown herpes encephalitis and the blood cultures showed a nocardia blood infection. Tragically, his body didn't have the immune system to fight it off.

Regardless of what was happening around me, I grew spiritually. I continued to journal, less frequently, but just as honestly as before. I poured out my fears and prayed on paper again.

January 16, 2004:

Psalms: Cords of death entangle me, the anguish of the grave came upon me, I am... no WAS... overcome by trouble and sorrow. Then I called on the name of the LORD! Oh, Lord, save me!!! You, oh, Lord, will deliver my soul from death, my eyes from tears, my feet from stumbling.

Isaiah: In quietness and trust is my strength. He rises to show me compassion. Blessed are all who WAIT for Him. They will weep no more. How gracious He will be when I cry for help. As soon as He hears, He will answer me. Do You hear me, God?? He will not grow tired or weary, and His understanding no one can fathom. He GIVES strength to the weary and increases the power of the weak. Those who hope in the Lord WILL renew their strength.

Luke: The disciples went and woke Jesus (in the storm). "Master, we're going to drown." Jesus rebuked the storm and said, "Where is your faith?!" Disciples freaked out in the midst of their storm even though Jesus was with them! They didn't use their faith. Jesus is with me RIGHT NOW. I have been freaking out. Where is my faith? Really, where? God, help me to fall onto You. I cry out to You, God.

My creator, my God, my love. I know You…help. What can I do? What should I do? Where do I go? God, the pain is so real in my heart.

I miss him so much. Fill this emptiness. Take the pain from my heart, my soul, and fill the emptiness with praise. Fill me with You. Please, Lord, come. It is so real, so real.

Pain fills my body with tears, sadness, anxiety, emotion. Fear – as this core of fear is spoken to – resisted – spoken to with the WORD of God, it starts to leave out of my heart and soul and into my hands. I can keep it or lay it down. I lay it down at Your feet, Jesus. Help me to not pick it up again. Help me, Jesus, to leave it with You and pick up You. Fill me anew with Your love, peace, mercy. Have mercy on me, Father. I beg for mercy. Fill me with praise. Praise to Your name, praise to Your holy name, singing praises to You.

I was only four days into the ICU stay and already so desperate. It was very hard to see Bob every day, sit by his bed every day, and still miss him. I missed his voice. I wasn't the only one.

I kept Bob's wallet and cell phone with me in my purse. Rusty called Bob's phone routinely. Every time I answered it, he said in a matter-of-fact tone of voice, "May I speak to Bob now?"

Every time I answered, "Not yet." It was a strange game we played that helped me to know that we were placing our hope in Bob's coming back. He would come back.

24
The Garden in the Middle of my Battlefield

It's weird how you settle into a sort of new life, a new routine. The hospital was my home. My actual house was just my resting spot. Work was irrelevant. Food was an afterthought. Each day was like a marathon. I'd wake up alive, rejuvenated, in a hurry. I'd stay all day and wait for Bob to wake up, but by the end of the day, I'd be back into that same argument with myself whether to go or stay.

Paula, Mary, and Katie took turns sleeping with me when I went home. I was convinced that I couldn't sleep alone. I remember very vividly the first night that I was alone. "I can do this. I don't need anyone. I'll be okay." I wrapped myself in my prayer shawl; Bob was covered with Hope's.

I told God, "You'll have to sleep with me tonight. I am not alone; You are with me. I can do this." As I lay there alone, wrapped in my prayer shawl, I heard God again.

"What if you lose him?"

Back to the garden. The garden – this time in shock. Here I am in the middle of a battlefield, and there is a garden? I'm here again. Hearing that voice in my head that I'd heard seven months before: "What if you lose it all? What if you lose him?"

This time the fight was against the enemy, not God. Last time I fought God. I told God, "No! I can't do this."

This time it was too late, it was happening. I wasn't fighting God; I was depending on Him.

"What if I lose him?" I sobbed out loud in my bed. I was repeating the question that I knew God was asking me.

I sobbed, cried, yelled back, "What if I lose him??"

I hadn't come to the point of sweating blood; if I could have, would I have? My garden again. It was my opportunity to completely and totally surrender my will to Him.

"Okay, if you need to take him… I don't understand why, but I'll be okay, God. Just please, please, please, please, God, don't You leave me! Don't ever leave me! I can only survive this with You by my side. It's okay, God, I'll be okay.

"Shhh, it's okay. I know I'll be okay. I don't understand, but I accept. You are God. You know best. If for some unknown-to-me reason, Aimie, Katie, and I need to live without Bob, we will. Promise You'll never leave me, God. I understand that You know more than I do. You are bigger than I am. You know that I'll be okay."

Not my will, but Yours be done. Is that what I was saying? Finally? I was broken. How is it that in the middle of this battle, I've found my garden again? There I was, another chance to lay down my needs, my wants, another chance in the garden.

This time I didn't argue with God. The "Shhh, it's okay" was that I was going to be okay. No matter what happened to Bob, I would be okay because God had me, so I gave my will to Him.

It may sound like a small thing, but it was my turning point. It may sound like an easy thing; if so, then you've never been to your garden. You've never completely surrendered your will to Him. It was so hard. It meant that I'd completely lost any control – not that I truly had control, but until that point, I thought I did. It was like I had been walking a tight rope. I had been trying to stay on that rope, using whatever I could grab onto for balance. When I finally let go, when I finally fell, there was a net to catch me. Why was I so afraid to fall into that net?

That night in my bed alone, I fell into that net. I let go, and I prayed that God would catch me and never let me go. I slept. I stopped crying, exhausted from this trip into the garden. I slept feeling the arms of God holding me. Last time I left the garden in Minnesota, at the Radisson, I'd walked into Bob's arms. He had held me, comforted me, convinced me that we'd be okay. As much as I missed Bob and his comfort, I knew that the arms that held me now were bigger and stronger than Bob's ever would be.

I would be okay.

I woke, as usual, before the sun, and called the nurse's station.

"Hi, this is Kim. How did Bob do last night?"

They replied as I had told them they would. Yes, I gave them all instructions of what to say to me when I called. "Bob had a great night!" They started with that no matter what really happened, then they'd fill me in on details of temperature spikes, urine output, creatinine levels, white count, etc.

When Jesus left His garden, He went to carry His cross. Was it time now to carry mine? There was a new rope to walk, a new cross to bear. This time I had a spotter, and I'd been in the net, so I knew it was there to catch me. It would be okay if I fell again; I wasn't afraid. I had a new sense of confidence. I knew that no matter what happened, I would be fine, so that gave me courage, courage to go back onto the battlefield. I was less afraid of the enemy, less afraid of death. The worst thing that could happen was Bob's death, and I had already accepted that if that was God's will, I'd be okay. However, if God didn't want him, I was going to fight anything and everything in hell if I had to to keep him. I think I did.

Back to the battle. Back to the hospital. Everything was different. I wasn't afraid anymore; I was a warrior. Ephesians talks about spiritual warfare. We do not fight flesh and blood, we fight powers and principalities of darkness. Well, I was going to fight them then. I wouldn't listen to the doctors.

The Book of Romans says "Let God be true, and every man a liar." (NIV Bible) I would speak to Bob's body from the word of God.

I was encouraged, I was renewed. I had a battle to fight, and I was not fighting blindly anymore. I had my eyes opened and was toe-to-toe with the evil forces of the enemy. I had the sword of the word, and I used it. I had the shield of faith, and I used it.

Still, the enemy is a worthy adversary. He wasn't finished fighting either, and he still had tricks up his sleeve.

Everything became strangely different, strangely clear. I saw people's strengths and weaknesses in their eyes. Some eyes were dark, fearful, confused… filled with the enemy. Some eyes were focused, clear… filled with fight.

I never again saw the angels that I saw the first night that Bob took his turn for the worse, but I saw other spirits. I saw them on people, in people. I knew what I was looking at. I stayed away from those people. I couldn't look them in the eyes, I wouldn't. I questioned every nurse, every therapist who entered the room: "Were they for us or against us?"

I had anointing oil from the church. I used this oil and wiped it on the door frame of his room. I prayed that God would anoint any person who walked through the door. I prayed that the evil spirits of the enemy would not come in as they were not welcome and had to stay away from Bob and his room. I commanded them to stay away from him. I anointed him and spoke healing over every cell of his body. I spoke into each of his hospital rooms and commanded that only God and His angels would inhabit those rooms. Where God and His light were, there could be no darkness.

The enemy was not welcome; we resisted him and his angels of darkness; and therefore, according to the word of God, they MUST FLEE. Where the light is, there can be no darkness. God's presence and God's Holy Spirit would usher in healing and chase away the sickness, disease, and fear of the enemy. We repeated these prayers like our battle cry, our anthem.

****

Gethsemane. Our opportunity to lay down our will for the Father's. The land of opportunity, the land of brokenness, the land of crucifixion. As we crucify our flesh in the garden, the spirit lives on. New birth. The spirit lives on. The fight with God, who's bigger? Who will win? He will. The opportunity to see that though He wins, He hands us the victory, the spoils of battle. You battle your own mind, your own will, your own flesh first. Then, when you lay it all down, leave it in the garden, you walk out changed. Don't pick it up again. Will we all face our opportunity in the garden in the middle of a battlefield? Are we all broken? As a jar breaks, the oil spills out. Everything in me was spilled out.

When I could pull away from the front lines briefly, I would pace an abandoned hallway, or find an empty "one seater" restroom and sing. I sang to God, I sang to myself.

"I'm gonna worship my King! I'm gonna praise His name! I'm gonna lift up holy hands, I'm gonna worship my King!"

I'd force myself to sing. Sometimes sounding angry, determined, anything but worshipful, but I CHOSE to worship. I made a conscious decision to do it.

"I'm gonna praise Him in the morning, praise Him in the night. I'm gonna worship my King!" Then I'd hear it, another voice; in my head, I heard it. Or was it in my spirit? Slowly, sweetly, so peacefully in the midst of my battle cry song, *"Take joy, my King... in what you hear."* It would always stop me in my tracks, I'd catch my breath and then break down into tearful singing with the voice, *"Let it be a sweet, sweet sound in Your ear."*

Such peace, such joy. That was it, one verse, never more, but that was all I needed, and I felt refreshed. The joy of the Lord became my strength. It was that strength that led me back onto the battle field, back into Bob's room.

Over a year later, I found a verse in the Bible that still makes me cry to read it.

Zephaniah 3:17 The Lord your God is with you; He is mighty to save. He will take great delight in you, He will quiet you with His love, He will rejoice over you with singing.

Thank you, God.

* * * * * * *

The transplant ICU was busy – business was good for cancer – and they needed his room. That's what they told me.

I felt like they were giving up on him. We're going to send him to the medical ICU on the second floor, is what they said.

"He doesn't need to be in isolation anymore because his white blood cell count is back to normal."

"He's not going to make it," is what I heard. "There's nothing more we can do for him here," is what I heard.

I knew how the hospital census worked. I knew that they sent the most critical patients to the ICU, and I knew that the BMT ICU was for the transplant patients, and Bob wasn't really even a transplant patient yet. It all made sense. However, I also knew that he'd get much better specialized care in the BMT ICU. Now we were going to regular medicine, the "catch-all."

It wasn't that bad really, but I had just gotten to the point where I could feel safe leaving at night. I knew the nurses, and I trusted them. They were so good to me.

"Do you need a hug?" they'd say. "Don't worry, we'll keep a good eye on him and call if there is any change at all. You need to get home and get some sleep then come back."

"Yes, Kim, we know the rules, keep the radio on all night, same station. When you call in the morning, tell you that he had a wonderful night. No bad news, got it."

Now if he moved, I'd have to "break-in" a whole new bunch of nurses. So be it.

On January 18th, he was moved to a new ICU. We left our living room, and our den, and we went to the next waiting room. We would spend twelve days there. Bob would lose his hair, start dialysis, start receiving all nutrition through an I.V. bag (TPN), and come off the breathing machine.

When the team of doctors told me that he was moving, I started to cry. Tim told me that it would be okay, that the same doctors would be overseeing his care and that the nurses were great.

"Is there anything I can do for you, Kim?" I watched as he put his hand on mine.

I raised my head and said, "Do you pray?"

"Yes, and I have been praying for Bob."

"Then that's all you can do. Just do your job to the best of your ability and pray for God to do His part. Thank you, Tim."

He was sincerely sorry.

Before Bob left the BMT ICU, we were introduced to a new doctor, a nephrologist. Dr. Richards, who was our regular nephrologist, didn't have privileges at this hospital, so we had to use one who did – Dr. Smith and his team of merry men. As far as I was concerned, they were sent by the enemy. Dr. Smith was called into see Bob due to his limited kidney function. He'd kept a close eye on him and had now decided that Bob's kidneys were failing, and he would need to go on dialysis.

I stood in our "den" and listened to the clinical description of this train wreck of a patient… oh, Bob. I quickly took in everything he'd said and didn't dwell on any one symptom too long. "We need to put him on dialysis," he stated slowly and watched as I took it all in.

"Okay. Do people sometimes have dialysis just for a period of time and then come off of it?" I didn't sound like a nurse. What kind of question was that? It was the desperate question of a desperate wife.

"It's possible," he said very slowly and carefully.

"Okay then. We'll have a little dialysis for awhile," I said as if I were planning something as frivolous as dinner.

"We'll do dialysis and then when the I.V. medication for the encephalitis stops, we'll stop the dialysis."

He let me hold on to that hope and shook his head while I signed the consent form.

****

Psalm 5:3 In the morning, O Lord, You hear my voice; in the morning I lay my requests before You and wait in expectation. (NIV Bible)

I started to get into some sort of routine. By routine, I don't mean normal, just patterns. Battle plans were being carried out. Hope had told me and others to wake before the dawn and pray. "Pray as the sun rises," she said. "It is very important. It will be a sacrifice, but do it."

Stan, Paula, Kathy, and Mary all set their alarms and woke every morning to pray before the sun came up. Hope was up during the night always. She took the night watch. We had people praying around the clock. Someone was ALWAYS praying. I didn't need an alarm. My body woke every morning before the sun. I woke every day with a start.

"Oh, God, I'm late! I have to get to the hospital! I can't leave him alone!" Every morning I felt late. I rushed out of bed, showered, dressed, and jumped in the car to leave. I raced to the hospital and only when I walked into the unit, did I start to calm. Deep breath. I'm here. Then the next wave of emotion would hit me as I walked through the door to his room.

"Oh, God, he's sick. Not Bob. He's not Bob."

Stop these thoughts. He is healed in Jesus' name. I would put my purse and bag down in my chair and prepare myself to come to his side. I would put my face in his and kiss him and tell him good morning. I would pick up the

"You Know You're a Redneck" calendar that his friend Scott had sent him and tell him the day, date, and then read the quote of the day.

I would tell him how many days he'd been in the hospital and then I'd tell him the appropriate date and weekday.

I tried to keep him oriented to where he was, some sort of time frame. Funny, I was trying to give him a time frame but had lost all sense of time myself. I said, "What is today?" a lot.

It never became easy to walk into the room and see him lying there, mouth hanging open, drooling, unable to hold his own head up, hospital gown soiled with his own secretions. He was a mess.

People would look at me and say, "You're doing so well, Kim, you're so strong!" I would fight the urge to jump on them and start hitting them and scream, "No, I'm not! I'm not doing well, I'm not holding it together, I'm not strong. I am weak! I am weak! I am weak!"

It felt so lonely, so incredibly lonely. Everyone was around, yet no one was there. I got up every day and went to the hospital. I followed that routine because somehow in it, I found comfort. The only thing that comforted me was sitting in that room every day. Waiting… waiting… waiting on Bob, waiting on God.

Somehow I knew that God would move. I waited for it every day next to Bob's bed. For two months I sat in that room with him. Leaving made me feel guilty. Leaving made me feel like I was giving up. Leaving was not an option. One day the dietician came into the room. It had to be February by then because it was our third room.

He said, "You're still here."

Though it was more of a statement than a question, I answered him, "Yes."

"Most people don't stay," he continued.

"Where else would I go?"

I couldn't understand what he was saying to me. Was he telling me to go? Was he telling me to give up? It was so strange.

"You can't imagine the amount of marriages that we see split up in cases like this. This is very difficult on a relationship."

We didn't have a relationship, we had a marriage. Marriage means that I stay here. Two becoming one, remember that? I wasn't going anywhere, I had nowhere to go. I was sticking it out. If it would have been nothing but a battle of persistence and perseverance, I would have won. I knew, though, that it wasn't my battle to win. It was God's.

25
Using Power of Attorney to Guard My Sacrifice

I completely trusted God to care for him physically. I knew that the physical condition that he was in was dire. I knew from my professional background, from my experience caring for train-wreck patients as we called them, from my common sense, that Bob's medical outcome looked bleak. I couldn't rely on the medical outlook. I couldn't rely on the drugs. I couldn't rely on the doctors or blood tests or treatments. I could only rely on God. He was my complete source. He would heal Bob – nothing else, no one else. I was giving it ALL to Him. I knew what tests were being run, and I knew what treatments were being tried. It didn't matter whether I agreed or didn't agree with the doctors; it was out of their hands. I even had some of the doctors tell me so.

"It's out of our hands, Kim." How clear is that?

Good, God had it: good for me, bad for Bob's family.

They hadn't given up or given in yet. Remember I had laid it all down to God.

They hadn't. They evidently saw that I had given up, but they hadn't seen that I'd given it over to God, that I had laid it all down, and I wasn't trying frantically to fix Bob anymore. They mistook the fact that I had laid it down for an opening to pick it up. They evidently saw me as sticking my head in the sand and thought that someone needed to take charge in my stead. What they didn't know is that I hadn't stuck my head in the sand. I had laid Bob's life down at an altar. I wasn't going to let anyone else step in and pick that sacrifice up. I guarded my sacrifice. I guarded my decision to let God take charge. I wasn't going to let someone else take over. It was so hard for me to not try to take charge; it was even harder for them to not take charge. That was their battle.

My sisters-in-law are also nurses. The family had family conferences often. I would sit in the waiting room and listen to them plan their next family meeting – who was cooking, who was bringing dessert or salad. They were going to get together and brainstorm what they should do. What could they do? They drank from the well of information poured out on the internet, they tasted the delicacies of knowledge from other doctors, they read and re-read any piece of literature they could get their hands on, all in the name of becoming more educated. Did it help? I don't know. I'll never know.

One day while trying to fill themselves up with knowledge, they asked the psychologist who had been assigned to Bob's case if they could have a special meeting with his doctor. They wanted more information. They requested that I not be in attendance. The psychologist contacted me and explained to me that they had requested this family meeting and also that they had requested that I not attend.

I felt like I had been stabbed. I felt like a balloon being deflated. My worst fears were coming true. Had they really tried to exclude me? The fact that I wasn't "one of them" was being made apparent again. I had prayed and begged God to see Bob and me as one during this time, to see us as one flesh, to truly develop the covenant relationship and see us as two who had become one. That was my life-saving prayer for Bob. If my faith could be forged to Bob's by our covenant marriage relationship, together we could stand through this, through all of it. We were one. His family didn't see it.

Before these events surrounding his family, I had only spoken to the psychologist once. Dr. Jeffries had introduced me to her the day after Bob was intubated.

"Kim, this is Dr. Siret.; she's the BMT psychologist. She helps people through some difficult times. I thought you'd like to meet her," Dr. Jeffries had stated.

"Hi, I'm okay. I'm going to be fine. Bob will be okay. I know you all think that I'm in denial, but I know exactly what's going on. I used to be a nurse. I realize the severity of his condition. I just refuse to accept it." I rambled on while she stared at me. "You see, I believe that the Bible is true, and I believe that the Bible says if you believe in faith, you can receive healing. So I'm not in denial, I'm just believing the Bible to be true. I have to have faith right now. This is the most important time for me to have faith. Don't tell me to lose my greatest coping ability right now when I need it most."

I believe I rambled on more… I don't know what I said.

She responded with, "You are going to be okay. You're coping just fine."

I thanked her for not telling me that I was going crazy. It would have been hard to hear that from a mental health professional. I was glad to get confirmation that I was not. This was the only time I spoke with her until she called about this meeting.

"What? Can they do this?" I asked Dr. Siret.

"No, they cannot. I explained to them that they cannot have a meeting with Dr. Jeffries without you in attendance. We'd like to schedule it for Thursday morning, and one more thing, do you have a power of attorney?"

The power of attorney that Bob and I had completed with Aimie and Paula was sitting at home in my briefcase. "Yes, I have one, why?"

"Can you bring it to the hospital? As soon as possible?"

My heart pounded in my chest; this wasn't normal. What was going on?

"Now?! Why, what's happening? Why do you need it?" I didn't understand, I couldn't fit this piece into the puzzle that was now my life.

"It's not emergent; just bring it as soon as you can. Tomorrow will be fine." She didn't sound scared, so why should I be scared?

"Can I bring my mom to this meeting?" I asked, and as I spoke, I could hear the fear in my voice, I realized that I was afraid to be alone with them.

"Of course you can. This is your meeting, Kim."

"It's not *my* meeting. I don't have any questions, but I will most certainly be there," I replied, hearing the fear in my voice ebbing away. A wave or courage was rising up in me.

* * * * * * *

I never knew why she asked for the power of attorney; I didn't ask. Some of the hospital staff alluded to what was happening.

When I brought it in that evening, I gave it to his nurse, "Dr. Siret wanted me to bring this in."

"Oh, yes, we've been waiting for this. Some family members are asking a lot of weird questions. They keep asking us who can read the chart, and I think they want a copy."

I knew from working in the hospital that family members asking us for copies of the chart usually wasn't a good thing. They were looking for something that usually ended up in litigation somewhere. As a nurse I was always a bit nervous around these families. I didn't want Bob's nurses to be nervous around us. I assured them that it was all okay.

She made copies of the form and gave me back the original. "I'm putting a copy in his chart and giving a copy to Dr. Jeffries for the cancer center chart, too."

January 23, 2004:

Bob has opened his eyes. He seems to know we're here at times. Right-sided hand squeezes and leg movement. Rectal tube and foley in place still. Making minimal to no urine. Started dialysis about four days ago. Tolerating well. Bowels have slowed to an almost stop, ilius? New rash to trunk area, bactrim? Otherwise same. Ventilator still on, lungs sound great, but he needs to wake more and prove to us that he can support his airway. He doesn't seem to be fighting the tube yet. Oh, God, help. I sleep alone now. It's hard. I want him back, but I don't know what kind of man I'll have back. That's okay. This is a journey between Bob and God. Bob will be a new man. Bob is a new man. I can't wait to hear the story being told by Bob. Where have you been, Bob? Tell us all about it. What did God do for you? What did He say? Bob's family planned a meeting yesterday. Dr. S. told me; I went. Sprung a few surprises on me.

I was so afraid to walk into that meeting. I was so afraid of them. Why? Because they hadn't let God take over yet? Because they were still looking to man for answers?

Because I had to sit and listen to the doctor explain again that Bob was very, very sick?

I had faced that, though. I knew that Bob was sick. I knew that Bob was by all odds not going to get better. I was okay with that because I had laid it all down to God. So why was I so scared? It was like an ambush to me. I felt like all of the secret family meetings had culminated into this one meeting. They had put their heads together, combined their knowledge and their opinions, and once and for all, they were going to get to the bottom of this. Bottom of what? I felt like they thought I was hiding something from them, but what could I have been hiding? They were so scared and so out of control they were just trying to gain some of that control back. They needed to know what was happening. Didn't we all?

The meeting was in our living room/waiting room. I asked my mom and Paula to come with me. I'd asked Stan, too, but he had an important meeting at work and couldn't make it. He'd been with me through so much, and I felt like I needed him. He was strong. It felt good when he was there. I was scared that he couldn't make it. I entered the room last. There was only one available seat, next to Dave.

"Thank You, God, that I'm sitting by Dave," I thought.

I didn't perceive him as being so "against" me. Andrea shared that couch with us. Steve and Susan sat on the love seat next to us. Marge, Kathy, and Mary sat at the table and chairs across from us. Steve, Sr. sat in a chair next to Marge, and Mom and Paula took their positions immediately to the right of me on the floor. I played with a piece of napkin, rolling it back and forth on the arm of the couch. Back and forth, back and forth. I spoke to God in my head, "I'll be okay. I won't say anything unless you want me to. Please slow my heart down; it's beating so rapidly. It's so loud. Can anyone else hear it?"

Dr. Jeffries was awesome. He thanked us all for coming and explained, for what I felt was the fifteenth time, how sick Bob was. He was professional, compassionate, and informative. That is, as informative as he could have been. He didn't have all of the answers. I think that's what Bob's family wanted, all of the answers. God held the answers; no man did. They were looking for that man who would tell them that he could fix Bob, still refusing that altar.

They asked question after question that had all been answered before.

Bob's mother asked, "Why did this happen to Bob?"

Dr. Jeffries explained that the chemotherapy and the steroids that they had used to treat the cancer had weakened Bob's immune system, and in his compromised status, he had contracted these infections.

"So you're calling this cancer then?" she asked.

WHERE HAD THEY BEEN?

"Yes." Dr. Jeffries was not as surprised as I was at the seemingly out-of-left-field question.

"Why do people get this kind of cancer? Why does Bob have this?" His mother kept asking the same questions that she had asked during Bob's diagnosis. "What caused it? How did he get it? Was it his job? Was it the food he eats? Was it genetic? Should everyone else be tested? Where did it come from?"

I felt like I knew… the enemy!! Hello! He has come to kill, steal, and destroy. He has brought disease with him. I don't accept it. Resist the enemy, and he must flee.

Dr. Jeffries didn't have an answer for her.

She persisted, "What do you tell people who get this?"

What he said was, "I tell them it's bad luck."

My mom swears that Dr. Jeffries said, "I tell them it's because God loves them." She almost fell over when he said it. No one heard that but her. She believes to this day God was talking to her. I believe it, too.

Bob's family continued to question Dr. Jeffries. I listened to the questions that I'd heard umpteen times and listened to the answers that I'd heard just as many times. I continued to roll my napkin along the arm of the couch. It was starting to resemble a flower with petals stemming out of the tightly-rolled column that was between my forefinger and the couch's arm. Huh! That was very nice of You, God, to show me a little beauty in the middle of this tough situation.

Eventually, the questions ended. "Is there anything else?" Dr. Jeffries asked, not in any way impatient with answering the same questions again.

Susan spoke to Steve, "I think we should tell him."

"Oh, okay," Steve replied to Susan, obviously waiting for her to tell him.

"Steve has gotten a ticket to fly to Florida to meet with a doctor. He has spoken with him on the phone and wants to go meet with him in person concerning Bob's condition."

It was very obvious that the whole family knew this plan and that they were springing it on Dr. Jeffries as if they were saying, "Since you don't know how to fix Bob, we're going to go talk to someone who does."

Dr. Jeffries responded with his usual confident professionalism.

"Oh, the national myeloma conference? That should be a good conference. I think they'll have some family support information.

Steve mentioned the doctor's name, and Dr. Jeffries responded, "I've never heard of him, but if you see Dr. McAdams there, tell him hello for me. He's the leader in the treatment and study of myeloma. He's the doctor who diagnosed Bob. Kim and Bob have met him."

Thank you, Dr. Jeffries. Thanks for letting them know that we did see the best, and the best doctor in the country, maybe the world, agrees with your treatment decisions. He was confident enough in himself and in his treatment of Bob that he didn't take this challenge personally; he understood it for what it was: a grieving family grasping for straws, a grieving family looking for an answer to a question that no man could answer.

In my battle stance, I saw the challenges as an attack. It was an attack again on the decision that Bob and I had made to choose this doctor, this hospital. I had learned that the doctor whom Steve was meeting was the same one that they had asked Bob to speak to back in December, the same one whom his father wanted him to talk to so badly that he gave Bob the piece of paper with his phone number on it on Christmas Eve while we were celebrating that the insurance had just approved Dr. Jeffries and the Denver transplant center. Wow, they must love this doctor. This was the "What would it hurt to get another opinion?" doctor. He practiced in California.

Steve had said, "If I ever butt in again, tell me to go to hell."

I didn't. After that meeting, I looked him in the eye and told him, "I hope you find what you're looking for."

I truly did. I hoped that he would find the answer. The answer was God. The answer was peace. Let all men be liars, and let God be true. God was true, God was truth.

Dr. Jeffries was finished; there were no more questions.

I rose from my seat and left the room as soon as Dr. Jeffries left. I didn't say much to anyone, I just had to get back to the second floor, back to Bob. As I was leaving, I heard Bob's dad say in a tone of disbelief, "I didn't realize he was this sick."

I felt sorry for him. Why were they so far behind us in this process?

My mom and Paula were close on my heels as I entered Bob's ICU cubicle again. There he was. Same Bob. I wanted so much for him to wake up just to calm me down.

"Bob, I need you!" I wanted to scream at him for what was happening, "Bob, I need you!"

I wanted to tell him that his family was treating me like an outsider again, that they were hurting me again, but what would he say?

The same thing as always: "They do care about you, Kim. Just ignore them."

I had the conversation in my head. I resigned myself to the fact that Bob would not want me to be feeling hurt, so I tried to let it go. I tried.

His family slowly trickled in to the second floor waiting room and came into the ICU begging their turns at his bedside. This ICU was much more strict with visiting hours. We were kicked out for two hours a day for shift change, and most of the nurses only allowed two visitors at a time. That suited me just fine. The room was small and trying to fit anyone else around the ventilator, dialysis machine, two I.V. machines and bedside tables was nearly impossible. We always felt like we were in someone's way in this cubicle. This was another reason to wish we were back in the BMT ICU.

Mom and Paula left the room to allow his family their turns. I didn't leave very often. I couldn't. It was adult separation anxiety. I had it bad.

His father and sister stood at the bedside and spoke to his appearingly lifeless body.

"Looking good today, Bob! You'll be out of here before you know it."

At least they were speaking positively to him.

His brother Steve showed up at the door, and a group of them congregated by the door way. As a nurse, I can remember hating when family members came into the unit and congregated to confer. I always made them go back to the waiting room. They were discussing who was going to take Steve to the airport. They belabored over the arrangements for what seemed like forever. I just didn't want to listen to it, and I didn't want it being discussed in front of Bob. The last time Bob's family had tried to push him into his seventh second opinion doctor, Bob had been so upset he couldn't sleep. I wouldn't let a hint of that doubt, that fear, that confusion enter into his room.

"Let's not talk about this here," I stated very quietly.

We all went outside in the waiting room. Everyone was there. They conferred again on who would take Steve to the airport, and finally he left for Florida.

26
Win - Win Situation

I don't remember how long Steve was gone. I remember sitting in the waiting room one day and listening to Bob's family talk to him on the phone, "Have you met him yet?"

God, help me. What were they looking for? So much energy was being wasted. Bob's father looked at me and said, "Steve has met this other doctor. He's on a first name basis with him already. He's gonna get to the bottom of this and straighten Dr. Jeffries out."

Was this some sort of challenge? Was he yelling *at* me? Was this my fault? I don't exactly know what response he was expecting from me, but certainly not what he got. I hummed. I thanked God for shutting my mouth because I had a few things that I wanted to say, but I just hummed. I remember it so vividly; I hummed the song, "Nothing but the Blood of Jesus." I continued to hum while getting up out of my chair and walking away. I heard his sigh of exacerbation over my shoulder. "That's okay, let him be mad at you," I said to myself. "Don't respond."

Things started to happen so quickly then. I don't exactly know the details, never did, never cared to. I believe that his family finally came to lay it down. They finally found the altar. I believe they found it after Steve came back from Florida. The day that Steve was coming back was a Sunday.

I sat next to a puzzle in the waiting room, and as I listened to them plan the meeting for that night, I made an announcement. I announced to them all: "Please don't talk about this meeting that Steve just had in front of Bob. It would kill him to know that Steve was going to meet this doctor. It would really upset him to hear it, and I don't want him to hear it, act like he was on a business trip." That is all I said. I had to say it. I didn't want anyone to tell Bob that they were doubting his doctor, doubting his care, doubting his treatment, doubting that he would get better.

I left the hospital to have dinner with my family, and while at dinner, his sister called me and asked me what was going on. I reiterated to her that I didn't want Bob hearing anything about this search for a new doctor again. The conversation was heated. It ended with something along the lines of her asking if I thought that they were trying to take control of Bob's care. I told her that was impossible because I had a power of attorney. There was silence. The conversation ended.

****

The next time I saw Steve, I asked how his trip was. He said it went very well and asked if he could speak with me. He and Dave sat across from me in the waiting room. They said that the doctor from California was at the conference in Florida. Steve had met with him and said that he would be interested in giving us another opinion. Steve said that the doctor needed to see Bob's records in order to give a better idea of what he would do to treat Bob, and he couldn't get Bob's hospital records without my approval.

"I know," I said. I waited to see if he had the audacity to ask.

He did. "Can we have your permission; can we have copies of his chart?"

"No."

"Kim, what would it hurt to get another doctor's opinion?" he asked, obviously confused as to why I wasn't going along with his plan.

I don't know what I said, but I remember feeling like I wanted to break down and cry. I felt as if I were holding on to God with every ounce of strength I had left, and if I let go for one brief second to look at another doctor, a man, I would take my attention off of God. I was so afraid that if I, for one second, even considered another option besides God, it would be showing a lack of faith. I could not risk that. I could not risk it. It was life or death now. I didn't have the luxury of questioning God. I didn't have the time to wander away from Him and see if there were something better! I needed to keep my attention where it was, and I couldn't allow this distraction to steal my attention. So I didn't. I emphatically rejected any request for his family to have copies of the chart.

I felt sympathy for his brother as I watched him try to convince me that it wouldn't hurt for them to try and find help from another doctor. I pitied the fact that he hadn't found what he was looking for yet, that he hadn't found peace, that he hadn't found God. He was still looking to man for the fix.

The meeting that I had with his brothers in the waiting room that afternoon was not the end of their trying to decide Bob's care, but it was a breaking point of sorts. There was a line drawn that day. I think they realized that we really did have different views of what was happening.

Dave paced, running his hands back and forth over the top of his head and said, "My parents just think that you're talking too much about God, you're just acting like God is going to take care of this. It really bothers them to hear you talk about it like that. Could you stop talking like that in front of them?"

"Stop talking about God?!" I asked incredulously. Dave quickly apologized as if for a moment he had lost control to someone else's line of questioning and realized in this brief moment that he didn't mean to ask that question.

"I'm sorry, Kim!" he quickly said to me.

I knew it. Dave had a good heart. He sincerely only wanted what was best for Bob; he just hadn't laid his burden down at the altar yet.

"Do you think you could at least just talk to this doctor from California and see what you think?" he hesitantly asked.

"No." The no's were coming easier. With every word that came out of their mouths, I was more and more convinced that this was an attack on our faith.

"Stand firm," I told myself. "Stand firm."

"Mom and Dad feel like they have no control," Steve said.

"They don't," my mom replied, "None of us do. Don't you understand that this is in God's hands now?"

No, they didn't.

"Could you at least arrange an appointment to talk to Dr. Jeffries again with my parents? Could you tell him to explain to them that he's an expert in this field? Maybe he could tell them about how good he is at his job, ask him to really talk himself up and make them confident that he knows what he's doing?" The last desperate attempt to help Mom and Dad see that this man was the right man to take care of their son.

"We already had a meeting with the doctor. What do you want me to say to him? Tell them you're the best?"

"Yes." They both agreed.

My mom told them, "Don't you understand that it doesn't matter if Bob is in the best or worst hospital with the best or worst doctor, if God wants him to live, he will. My mother was in Barnes hospital with one the country's most renowned heart surgeons operating on her, and she died on the operating table. He was the best. It didn't matter. And my brother-in-law was in a po-dunk, understaffed, little hospital in Illinois and had an aneurysm burst, and he should have died but lived. It's all in God's hands!"

Were they starting to listen, were they getting it?

January 25, 2004:

Rusty called me and said, "I know the battle has been won in Bob and his body. Don't let the battle with his family steal the victory. Bob would tell you to ignore this. He would put one hand up, push it away and say, 'Ah, don't let it bother you.' Let this be a win/win situation. Win on both fronts."

Everyone speaks to me like I'm in a battle.

About three hours after the call with Rusty, my estranged brother Mike called. He said, "You don't know how hard this is for me to call you. I don't want to talk to you, but I know I have to. I've been praying lately, and I feel like God is telling me something. I keep hearing "win/win situation." I know that I'm supposed to call you and tell you that, I know I am, and I don't know why. That's all." I couldn't believe what I was hearing.

"Have you spoken to Rusty?" I asked.

"Not in over a year," his voice was monotone. He had no idea what he had just said to me. Did he know that he had delivered confirmation of a word directly from God??

Praise You, God!! Praise You, God!! Thank You, God!!

Mike hung up, I cried.

Got to the hospital today, and Bob was awake!! Looking at me. He whispered something. Joy! Joy! Joy!

It's only been two weeks since this horror started. Feels like a lifetime. Two weeks since I've heard my husband speak to me.

27
Calling Bob Back

    In the midst of these meetings with Bob's family and another meeting with the psychologist, I missed writing something in my journal. I missed writing that Bob had been extubated. The pulmonary doctor was slowly weaning Bob from the breathing machine, and eventually one morning (before I had come in), she pulled the tube and Bob had started breathing on his own. The distraction of the family division had consumed my thoughts and my prayers so much that my journal doesn't even mention the miracle of Bob breathing again! I remember the day. I remember walking into the second floor ICU waiting room with Mom and Hope, and I said, "I'm going to go to the restroom before I go in to see him." Mom and Hope went in to see him while I was in the restroom but quickly came back out to the waiting room. I could hear them talking from the restroom; something had happened. I walked out of the restroom and my mom said, "Go! Go in and see him now!" very excitedly.

    I walked through the heavy wooden double doors and turned left to walk past the nurses' station and to his cubicle. Tim and Joey were sitting behind the nurses' station smiling at me. What was going on? As I turned right into the cubicle, I saw what they were all so excited about. There was Bob with NO TUBE, NO VENTILATOR! He lay there quietly breathing on his own. I was so excited I jumped back away from the door to his room, put both hands over my face and started to cry. Tim and Joey came over to me beaming, "Dr. Peterson extubated him this morning, he's doing great. Are you okay?" I was better than okay.

Just because the tube came out does not mean that he woke up. He didn't. At times he opened his eyes and stared at us or would follow my movements with his eyes, but not consistently. We didn't know what his mental status would be yet.

What we did know is that he was not out of the woods. His kidneys were worsening, and the dialysis went from every third day, to every other day and eventually to every day. He was receiving total parental nutrition (I.V. vitamins and minerals and fat) due to the fact that it had been so long since he'd had any nutrition.

Dr. Jeffries still visited every day. As did Tim, Joey and Jeff. Other doctors started coming in, too. It seemed like a new doctor every day. They would come in and introduce themselves and ask a litany of questions. Sometimes the thought that he was getting better would strike me as such a lie. "Look at him," I'd think. "Even if he doesn't die, he's going to be a vegetable." Many days I would start to believe that lie, believe that he was going to die.

I found solitude in the bathroom down the hall. "STOP IT!" I yelled at myself. "CALM DOWN!" I yelled at the fear, "I will not bow to you, fear, I will not! Satan, I hate you. God does not give me a spirit of fear, so it must be coming from you, Satan! I resist you and you MUST FLEE. God said so!! You dirty rotten son of a #*@ %!, do you know who you're messing with? I'm a child of God! I'm a child of the KING! I know Jesus. You remember Jesus? He died for me and ROSE FROM THE DEAD defeating you!! He lives in me. He intercedes for me. He is my strength. The same power that rose Jesus Christ from the dead lives in me! You don't even know the power that is in me! You cannot win!! You go back to hell where you belong and leave me and my family alone!"

One morning at 5:00 A.M., Hope called me, "Is Katie awake?"

"I don't know, why?"

"Wake her up. I have to come over; I've been up praying all night and need to talk to you both. I'm on my way. Have Katie open the door; you stay in bed. Don't get up until I get there."

I called Katie and she came to my room, "What's wrong?" she asked.

"I don't know; you know Hope. She has something she's been praying about, she needs to tell us, so go open the door."

Hope came into my room and sat next to me. "I've been up praying all night, and while praying I saw Bob. He has made a choice, and he will live. I saw a beautiful golden light around him; it wasn't too bright, but golden, and it was glowing. I didn't hear anything but knew that he saw the light and that he is going to come back to us. It's going to be incredibly hard for him to come back. Do you understand?"

I didn't.

"He will have to fight to come back. He's in a place now that he doesn't have to fight, but to get back to us, he will fight. Can I talk to Katie?"

Katie came into the room and Hope told her, "Honey, you are the voice to call him back. He needs to hear you, your voice. When he hears you talking to him, he will come back."

Katie and I stared at each other. We had no idea what she was talking about. "Okay," is all that Katie said.

Hope left. She looked exhausted. Whether she was exhausted from delivering that message to us or from being up all night praying, I didn't know.

That evening Katie came to the hospital. She came into Bob's cubicle and stood next to him. We were on either side of the bed. Stan and Kathy were in the room, too. Katie looked at Bob and spoke. "Hi Bob, it's Katie."

The most amazing thing happened. I didn't expect it to happen like this, neither did Katie. Bob rose up out of the bed. Head and shoulders off the pillow, left arm reaching across his body and right arm reaching up toward her. He grabbed her around the waist and pulled her toward him. It frightened her; it frightened me. Everyone in the room started to cry. She had called him out. It was the first time since Bob had been intubated that he had moved on his own. And it was no small movement! It looked as if he'd "woken up."

I sucked my breath in and cupped my hands over my mouth. It wasn't that I didn't expect Bob to wake up one day; I just really hadn't expected it to be so drastic. Hope was right, Katie's voice called him back. We called the nurses in to see him. We told the nurses, the doctors, our families, Hope. We told everyone. Bob was coming back.

January 29, 2004:

Still lots of doctors, lots of therapists; dialysis. Bob opens his eyes now. The nurses comment on how pretty his eyes are. I know, it's nice to see those eyes. Sometimes I wonder if he is comprehending any of this. He looks lost. His eyes open but look so empty sometimes. God, is he in there? I came to the hospital late today, about lunch time. I'm so tired. I called the nurses this morning, and they told me that he would be having dialysis early today. So I came afterwards. Bob was awake and alert when I arrived. Very responsive today. He followed me around the room with his eyes. I was drained. Tired physically, tired mentally, tired of coming to this hospital, tired of all of it. Not angry, not sad, just tired. Seeing him watch me helps. Seeing him try to talk, try to communicate with me is nice, very nice. Rejuvenates me. He was awesome today. He winked at me! He smiled, even tried to pucker his lips up for a kiss. I love him. I love God.

Dr. Trevor came in today and said, "I take it you have a little faith. Keep praying. It will be a long road of rehab, but I'm encouraged that he'll be fine. He's already really impressing me that he's made it through this far. Now it's up to God and Bob. We've done all we can do." As he said, "It's up to God and Bob," he walked over to Bob and placed his hand on Bob's chest as if to tell him that.

I felt as if an angel had just walked through the room. Thank You, God, Thank You for encouragement. Thank You for talking to me through Dr. Trevor.

* * * * * * *

After Bob woke up, Dr. Jeffries ordered that he have physical therapists come in and exercise his limbs and try to get him up into the chair. I took this as a sign of hope. They really were thinking of rehabilitation! He would live. The therapists came into the room and passively exercised his legs and arms. As I sat and watched the two therapists put Bob into a chair, I was amazed at the amount of muscle atrophy that had occurred. I had assisted the nurses with bathing him, but hadn't seen him sitting up in two weeks. When they sat him on the side of the bed, I cried at the sight. Every rib traced its way through the pale skin that covered him. His spine looked as if it were protruding through his back; his shoulders looked like softballs covered tautly with skin. He was a skeleton of a man. Oh, God, help me! He was so determined to sit up but couldn't hold his own torso up. He'd have a long way to go.

As soon as his monitors would start alarming that his oxygen saturations were dropping, the therapists knew it was time to stop. They would push him to this point every day. The alarms told us when he was tired because he still couldn't talk. He probably wouldn't have stopped us anyway. Although he was unable to communicate with us, it was obvious that he was determined to do what he was told. He could understand what they told him. We would watch as the therapists would tell Bob, "Lift your right leg." We watched his eyes and knew he was processing what he was told. Ten seconds or so later he would strain to lift his right leg. While he was barely clearing the bed, we would all clap and cheer! "Good, Bob! Awesome! Good job!" My mom said that we cheered so much when he did anything we were going to have a hard time stopping ourselves when he came home.

Everything with the family sort of calmed after the storm. His sisters went home to their families, and his parents went back to St. Louis to get their belongings and their van. Bob was obviously starting to show us all that he had no intention of dying. The road before us was a long one, we knew we had a long course of rehab ahead of us, but we were optimistic. We were all in it together.

****

Near the end of January, Dr. Jeffries came into the room and told me how happy he was with Bob's progress and gave us wonderful news. The BMT ICU had opened another bed, and they were going to take Bob back. It was such wonderful news for so many reasons. The rooms in the BMT unit were so much bigger and nicer and more accommodating for family members to be there, the nurses were so involved and compassionate (not to take anything away from the ICU nurses), and last but most certainly not least, it meant to me that Dr. Jeffries was seeing some hope in Bob's condition. He wasn't writing him off. He was taking him back under his wing. We were going to be back on the transplant team.

We moved Bob back the Friday before Superbowl. We were excited because we were going to come to the hospital and watch the game. We would watch from the waiting room and his room. It was going to be a big day for him, so we thought.

28

Super Bowl Seizure

February 1, 2004:
Superbowl Sunday
Bob had 2 grand mal seizures. Depakote levels down and fever spiked to 103.1. God, this is so hard. Hard. So hard.

I came to Bob's room Sunday after church. He seemed distant. Not that he'd ever completely come back to us, but his eyes seemed distant. He stared a blank stare. I put my face near his and said, "Bob, are you okay? Can you hear me?" He just stared. My heart started pounding. Something was wrong. I called the nurse and told her that something was not right.

This was her first time taking care of Bob.

"Tell me what you mean," she said. "I'm not as familiar with him as you are."

"Since waking up, he's been more and more alert. Like he follows me with his eyes, you know?" I told her. "This morning he looks distant. Just not there." The nurse took his vital signs and started a neuro exam. Bob's dad and mom entered the room for the big football game.

"Hello, Robert! Ready for the game?" We all talked to him like he was going to answer us at any moment. He never did.

I told Bob's parents that he was not looking right today. They stood at the foot of the bed and watched the nurse examine him.

Bob's lips started to twitch almost like it had that day in the car on the way to the hospital. "Look, he's trying to say something!" his dad said.

Oh, God!

"No, he's having a seizure," I blurted out nervously looking across the bed at the nurse. She looked at me with confirmation in her eyes, pressed the nurse's call light and said, "Page someone now!" She laid the head of Bob's bed flat and told me, "I'll be right back," as she rushed out of the room.

"He needs quiet," I spoke out loud to no one as I turned off the lights and closed the blinds.

Bob's parents disappeared out the door. "We'll go in the waiting room until you're finished."

I stood next to him and put my hands over his eyes, "Close your eyes, Bob, sleep." When I put my hand on him, I realized he was burning up. The nurse came back in, and Bob's foot started pointing down and his hands started to curl into fists, his eyes rolled back into his head, and he started to convulse. I backed away as the room filled with nurses and doctors. Not again! Not again! Not again! He was getting better! What was happening?

The nurse pushed I.V. Ativan, and Bob eventually stopped seizing. I sat across the room on the edge of my big chair and watched him. Slowly the room started to clear, only the nurse and one other person was left, and Bob started to seize again. The room filled again, and I paced back and forth crying. Was this it? Had we been fooled into thinking he was going to get better just for this? They pushed more Ativan, and he calmed again. They inserted Tylenol suppositories into his rectum to try to reduce his fever. They drew blood, they cultured urine, stool, blood, saliva, and the newest site for infection, a bed sore. He had developed a large bed sore on his tail bone. They were looking for a site of infection. What was causing this fever? They assumed the fever had caused the seizure, so we needed to break the fever, but where was it coming from?

Bob remained in a coma-like state the rest of the afternoon and evening. As his family and mine gathered in the waiting room for what we thought was going to be a football game, it became a waiting game. Family members were confused and angry that Bob seemed to be taking a turn for the worse again. Emotions were high. I was numb, completely numb. Why was this fight so relentless? My mom came into Bob's room and read aloud from her Bible at his bedside. She read for hours. Out loud. She would not stop. No matter who came into the room, doctor, nurse, family member, therapist – she stayed. Diligent. I sat across the room in the chair and stared at him. I was waiting for his eyes to open, wondering if they would. Family members took turns coming in; Hope was there, too. Stan called at noon to check in; he was in D. C. with Lisa and her family.

He sounded more exhausted than I. "Kim, how is Bob?"

"Not good, Stan. He had a couple of seizures this morning and hasn't regained consciousness yet." I started to cry.

He cried, too, I don't know if it was from my news or his, "Lisa's mom died this morning."

Oh, God! I felt like we were being pounded from every side, pounded into the ground.

Stan and I cried together for a bit. We had nothing else to give each other.

"I'm sorry," I said.

"I know, me, too," he replied. "Kim, I had kind of a dream last night right before she died. I saw her in a golden light. Like it was glowing…"

I stopped him. "Stan! Wait, I've heard this before." I called Hope to the phone, and she spoke to Stan. They agreed that they'd seen the same golden light in their dreams. What did this mean? Was Bob going to die? Hope seemed encouraged by it all. I just held on to the fact that she was encouraged. After all, she was the one who'd seen it, so I'd let her interpret it.

I will never forget the reaction of his brother Dave to Bob's Superbowl seizure day. He walked into the room, and without speaking a word to anyone, immediately dropped to his knees next to Bob's bedside and placed his left hand on Bob's chest and his right hand on Bob's thigh. He bowed his head and began to pray for his brother. The only noises in the room were the soft worship music that continued 24/7, and the bleep of the monitors overhead. We all stopped what we were doing and silently watched as Dave unashamedly shared the most intimate moment with God, his brother, and those of us in the room. I began to cry and walked into the bathroom to hide it from everyone. I was overtaken with emotion. I wasn't scared; I was amazed. To see Dave drop to his knees and lay hands on his brother like that was the most awesome display of brotherly love I think I've ever witnessed. I am honored to have shared it with them.

He did not open his eyes again until 2:30 A. M. I heard him stirring in the bed. I jumped up. "Bob?" I whispered into his face.

He opened his eyes and looked at me. Really looked at me, no vacant stare. I laid my head on his chest and cried, "Bob, is this too much for you?" I looked into his eyes to make sure he understood what I was saying. "Bob, are you still up for this fight? If you don't want to fight anymore, it's okay, I'm going to be okay. I will do whatever you want. Do you want to quit fighting now?"

He just stared at me, not vacantly. His eyes went back and forth and around my face, looking at me. I knew he understood what I was saying, "Bob, can you still do this? Do you understand what I'm saying to you?" He moved his left hand toward me, and I grabbed it with mine. He lifted his chin up and puckered his lips to me. I kissed him. He smiled with his eyes and nodded his head ever so slightly. He was staying with me. We were going to continue this fight. God, give me strength. I can no longer fight by my own power. I am completely spent.

February 3, 2004:
Happy 19th birthday, Aimie. We love you.
I bought Aimie a card today. Put a pen in Bob's hand and made him write his name. Had to help A LOT, but he did.

Though the seizures had stopped, the doctors continued to try and figure out what was causing the fever. They had weekly multi-disciplinary conferences regarding Bob's condition. The first week in February, after one of these morning conferences, I received a phone call from Dr. Jeffries. It was approximately 8:00 A. M., and I was in my car alone driving to the hospital.

"Kim, we've just finished our morning conference regarding Bob's condition. Dr. Peterson, Dr. Trevor, Dr. Butler, Dr. Siret, Dr. Smith and I have all put our heads together about these fevers. Kim, we think that Bob needs a tracheostomy. We'd like your consent to give him one.

"We believe the fevers are coming from pneumonia. Bob doesn't seem to be clearing his secretions, and we think he's aspirating on his own saliva again." He continued.

I had to pull over. Once I was safely parked, I tried to comprehend what was happening. I believe I started to cry, "A trach?"

"Kim, I know how hard this has been."

"I feel like we're going backwards!" I interrupted, and I know I was crying at this point. Another blow. How long, how long could we go on?

"We are not going backwards, Kim. This is just to help with his airway. He needs this to help clear his lungs. It doesn't have to be permanent." He was very compassionate and making a very logical medical point. I was just so sick of hearing all of these logical medical arguments.

"I know, I know! It's just so hard." I didn't have to be convinced. "I understand. This is not going backwards; this will help him." I wanted him to understand that I was not irrational, just tired.

"I'll see you when you get here, and we'll sign consents."

"Okay, I'm on my way." I hung up and laid my head on my steering wheel and cried. I tried to be logical, I tried to tell myself that a pulmonary specialist, a neurologist, an infectious disease specialist, a nephrologist, an internal medicine team, and a bone marrow specialist were all in agreement that this was the best treatment. Therefore, it had to be. I just couldn't get past the fact that we were suffering another blow from the enemy. I didn't think I could stand anymore. Medically speaking, I knew that Bob needed a trach or he was going to wind up either dying of pneumonia or going back on a ventilator. But emotionally speaking, I couldn't handle another procedure. But I would, and he did.

I pulled myself together and pulled out of the parking lot. I would go to the hospital and sign consents, plan for the next round and fight again no matter how tired I was. Bob was still up for the fight, so I was, too. No strength in me, but I'd fight with whatever I had.

I signed the consent forms for the trach and also for a J-tube to be placed in his stomach. Since it had been more than three weeks since Bob had eaten anything, they were going to start him on tube feedings. The dietician had been following his nutritional needs closely, and he had vacillated between Total Parental Nutrition (all I.V. nutrition) and Naso-Gastic tube feedings. They decided that it would be best if Bob had a tube surgically placed in his belly to be fed through. They would implant it at the same time they put the tracheostomy tube in his neck.

I called everyone and told them the next step on our journey. Bob's family overreacted. They decided that he didn't need a trach and tried to convince me of the same. They printed information from the internet and handed it to me trying to convince me not to let the doctors perform the procedure. They tried to explain to me what the procedure entailed and every adverse side effect of the procedure. Prior to being an oncology/bone marrow transplant nurse, I had been an ear, nose, and throat nurse. I had taken care of tracheostomy patients and worked as charge nurse in an ENT ICU taking care of post-op tracheostomy patients. I was well versed on what a tracheostomy was. I tried to explain to them that I understood what was happening, but they wouldn't listen to me.

I was very aware of how sick Bob was. I was completely aware of what was happening medically and physically. I also had another awareness: a spiritual awareness. Bob's spirit was safe.

The surgery was going to have to wait until Bob had been off of his anti-coagulation therapy long enough to allow his blood to begin to clot normally again. This meant that we would have to keep Bob's respiratory status as healthy as possible until then. The pulmonologist was concerned that Bob's oxygen saturation was slowly declining due to the pneumonia and compromised lung status. The morning before the surgery, she came into his room and threatened to put Bob back on the ventilator if he couldn't bring the oxygen saturation of his blood up on his own. My mom and I became determined to do our jobs as nurses and help Bob stay off the ventilator this last twenty-four hours. We asked the nurses if we could have help getting him up to a chair. We kept him up; we had him take deep breaths every hour. We kept him off the ventilator.

After Bob had the tracheostomy tube and J-tube placed, he had a complete turn around. The tracheostomy tube allowed the nurses to insert a suction catheter into his bronchial tubes and suction out sputum that was infectious. The sputum was cultured, and they detected pseudomonas that was determined to be the cause of the pneumonia and most likely the fevers that had eventually caused the seizures on Superbowl Sunday. Now that we had a bug to fight, they changed the antibiotics to more specifically fight the pseudomonas.

Bob's condition rebounded. Fast! Physically and mentally he was coming around. Within two days of having the surgery, he started walking across the room with the help of two physical therapists. Speech therapists worked with him to help him learn to communicate again. He slowly started writing on a dry erase board that we'd brought in. The spelling was atrocious, but we eventually started communicating again. The very first comprehensible sentence that Bob wrote to us was, "I need a sandwich!" So typical. My mom and I laughed so hard. Bob was hungry! He was definitely coming back.

The next three weeks were physically demanding on Bob. He was fighting to rehabilitate muscles that had atrophied. He was learning to use his mouth and tongue again. He was being "potty trained" because he had lost control of his bowels and bladder for so long. He was learning to exercise cognitive abilities in order to think again.

On February 6th, after the therapists had walked him across the room and back, they congratulated Bob and encouraged him to sit down on the bed. I was standing in front of him. He wouldn't sit. He raised his head and looked at me, put his arms out towards me, and pulled me close. He hugged me before he sat down. I felt like God himself was wrapping Bob's arms around me. I cried and thanked Him. He was going to be my husband again.

29
Beautiful Urine

We commanded by the word of God that every organ, tissue, and cell of his body would function in the perfection in which God had created it to perform. We forbade any sickness or disease to remain. We believed what we were praying.

One day when the dialysis technician arrived, she gave me a booklet about dialysis as an outpatient. I asked her what it was for.

She said, "If your husband continues to improve, he'll eventually be going home, and you'll want to know about some options for outpatient dialysis."

"He's not going home on dialysis," I told her.

"What? Who told you that?" she asked incredulously.

"God. We have faith. God hasn't brought him this far to not finish the job. His kidneys are going to start working again." I was so confident that I handed her the booklet back.

"I have to give that to you," she said as she handed the booklet back. "Keep it, just in case."

I threw it away when she left. Not in Bob's room where it would be a reminder of what she'd said, but outside.

On February 11th, I told Dr. Jeffries that I was concerned with the fact that Bob continued to have dialysis every day. "It takes so much out of him, he's so tired when it's over, and it takes up three hours of his day. He could rehab so much quicker if he could stop the dialysis." I was so convinced that his kidneys were healed I thought that they were hurting him with the dialysis. He told me that he would send the kidney specialist in to talk with me.

Dr. Smith was not as convinced as I was that Bob's kidneys were able to function. We argued for fifteen minutes.

I asked, "How do you know that his kidneys won't work? Take him off of dialysis and watch."

He was flabbergasted with me. "You don't understand! His blood work is showing that his kidneys are still not functioning."

"But if you take him off of the dialysis, they'll start working!" I argued with no factual basis but with the conviction of my soul.

"It doesn't work like that!" He raised his voice at me.

"It will for him. How do you KNOW it won't? What if you just cut back to every other day?"

We were at a stale mate. Neither of us were budging. He looked at me like I was a nut case who wouldn't listen to reason. I looked at him like a man with no faith.

He picked up Bob's chart and slammed it down on the counter. I stepped back a bit.

"He's getting too much fluid to stop dialysis; we're still pulling off almost eight pounds of fluid per day. If we stop, he'll blow up like a balloon!"

"No, he won't. He'll start peeing," I had an answer for everything.

"He will go into electrolyte imbalance," he was stating every scientific reason he could cite.

"Not if he starts producing urine! Can't you just skip one day?" I was arguing with him. I was not going to let him win.

He stormed out of the room. My heart was pounding. My mom and I looked at each other and shrugged. What did that mean? Were we stopping dialysis?

Dr. Jeffries came in later that day and pulled me out in the hall, "I hear you and Dr. Smith had quite a discussion."

"You mean argument? Did he tell you we argued?!" I started to get worked up again. I was ready to argue the point all over again.

"Yes. You must have been quite convincing. We're holding dialysis tomorrow to see what happens."

PRAISE GOD!

"Okay God, now You have to move. You have to prove Yourself. You have to show Yourself, God, You just have to." I begged God to show up and show off! Show them all, God! I prayed for Him to please back me up here, to back up my faith. We continued to lay hands on Bob and command his kidneys to work.

One day of no dialysis turned into two days, then three. Bob's foley bag started filling with urine. It was the most beautiful urine I'd ever seen. Everyone who came in the room commented on it.

"Look at that gorgeous urine!" The nurses would joke as they came in.

"I know! Don't you just love it?!" I'd say.

On Valentine's Day, the nurses collected all of Bob's urine for twenty-four hours to send to the lab for a twenty-four hour creatinine clearance. This test was going to determine how well his kidneys were clearing the impurities from his body. His blood tests were slowly coming back to normal, and he was slowly producing more urine, but they wanted a more accurate test.

I told them, "You know before we even came into the hospital, his kidneys were already damaged by the disease. He was walking around with seventy-five percent kidney function. I'd be happy with that."

The result came back. Bob's kidneys were functioning at one-hundred percent! Praise God!

To celebrate, I helped Bob take his first shower. The physical therapist helped me walk him into the bathroom, and we sat him on a shower chair. It had been five weeks since he'd been in a shower. It made me feel good for him. Afterwards, I dressed him in real clothes. Today was a banner day, so today was the day for real clothes. After showering and dressing, he sat in a chair, and we played cards: War. He was very slow but accurate. Handling the cards was difficult for him, but we were actually interacting. One of the nurses came in and said, "Kim, there's a delivery for you in the waiting room."

"What? What kind of delivery?" I didn't understand. Bob and I looked at each other.

"Just come with me," she hurried out of the room. We walked out into the waiting room, and there on the table was the most beautiful vase of red roses. The card read, "Have I told you lately that I love you? Bob."

I sat down and cried as I read the card. I looked at the nurse; she was crying, too.

"How did he do this?" I asked her.

"I have no idea!" She said, "We were all wondering that ourselves. That husband of yours is good!"

"But he can't talk. He can't even communicate. How…" I couldn't figure it out. I went back into his room to ask him. I showed him the card. He looked confused.

"Bob, did you do this?" He shook his head then pointed at his dry erase board.

He wrote "Rusty Stan." He was telling me that it was one of my brothers. I called them. Stan denied it.

Rusty said, "Bob did it. Boy, that guy is good, huh?" Rusty had sent me roses for Bob. "He never misses a Valentine's day; I didn't want him to miss this one." It was a perfect Valentine's day.

Three days later, on February 17th, Dr. Smith's associate came into Bob's room.

"I'm not going to promise you that you'll never have dialysis again, but you aren't going to have it anymore this hospitalization. We're going to pull that dialysis catheter out of your chest now."

Bob was standing at the bedside. We were just getting ready to walk with the therapists, and he reached out and grabbed the doctor and hugged him. I jumped up and down and said, "Praise God! Praise God! Praise God! I knew it!" Dr. Smith never came back to see us.

The rest of the tubes came out, too. No more catheters, no more I.V. fluids. The only tubes left were the tracheostomy tube in his throat and the J-tube that he was being fed through. The doctors and nurses started to spend less time with us. We started to spend more time with the speech and physical therapists. Dr. Jeffries discharged Bob from the BMT Unit.

"Bob, you're not my sickest patient anymore. As a matter of fact, I'm going to send you to the rehab floor, so they can get you ready to go home."

Bob spent a week on the rehab floor. He worked with the therapists four hours a day. He did math and word problems and began to write full sentences on his dry erase board. He needed less and less assistance. He became more and more aware. One day he wrote a long note to me before I arrived. When I came into the room, he handed me the note.

"You are so wonderful and beautiful. I am so lucky to have a wife like you. Thank you for everything you've done for me. I love you."

"You're welcome. I love you, too." Thank you, God. He's going to be my husband again.

He then wrote, "What happened to me? How long have I been here?"

I laughed. "Oh, Bob! You wouldn't believe it all if I told you. You are a miracle."

"How long?" He wrote again, "Two weeks?"

"It's been almost seven weeks, Bob."

He opened his eyes wide and sat straight up in the chair. "Seven???" he wrote.

"How have you kept it all together?" he wrote.

"You think I'm together?!" I laughed. "God has taken care of us, Bob."

He was very quiet for a long while. I think he was trying to digest what was happening. I had to explain the tracheostomy tube to him. He kept wanting to blow his nose, and I tried to get him to look in the mirror and wipe the secretions from his trach tube instead. I told him that he was breathing from the hole in his throat, not his nose and mouth. He was very confused. He wanted to drink. He became adamant about having a drink of water. The speech therapist wouldn't clear him to drink, though. He became angry with them. He had shown so much progress yet still had so much more to accomplish.

February 23, 2004:

Bob is asking so many questions now. Everything is going along now. The doctors and nurses have better looks on their faces when they come in. The visits are shorter, but it's still a long way to go for us. I wonder how life got to be this way. How can I sit and watch a miracle occur, watch Bob walk out from death, and then be angry? Have I held it together for so long, and now it's all going to fall apart? Now is when I'm going to blow? Don't let me, God. Please help me, Father. Help me to keep it together now as You did then. Hide me in that secret place again. Hold Your hand over me to protect me. Help me, Lord, not to be angry. Help me to forgive; don't let me be offended. How do you forgive someone who hasn't even asked for forgiveness? Love. God's love. Rusty called, "God gives you just enough for each day." Like manna from heaven. He also said, "The flood comes before the harvest."

30
Home Health

On February 26, 2004, Bob had his tracheostomy tube pulled and was discharged from the hospital. Dr. Peterson came into the room, pulled his trach tube out, placed a dressing over the hole in his neck and said, "Say hello."

"Hello," he hoarsely said. I broke down and cried. My mom cried.

Bob smiled; Dr. Peterson laughed.

"Say something else," she said.

"Something else," he said.

"I can't believe it!" I was overwhelmed. "These are the first words I've heard him say in seven weeks!" We packed up his room and took him home. It felt so good to have him in the car. He went home with a dressing on his neck that we would change for three days then the hole would close on its own. We had medication to apply to his slowly shrinking bed sore. We had a J-tube to care for and feed him through. We had seizure medication, anticoagulants, antibiotics for the nocardia infection, antiviral medication for the viral encephalitis, tube feeding supplies, and adult diapers for his frequent incontinence. We were just happy to be going home. We called off any and all visitors and slept for two days. I woke in the middle of the night to check on his breathing and took his pulse.

After we slept for the first two days, it was time to call the doctors' offices and schedule Bob's many visits. We set up home health nursing, home health speech, and physical therapy. I had to get back to work. My mom came over in the morning and stayed with him until I got home from work. Work was unbearable.

Bob was home, and everyone was looking for the relief of, "Good, they're back, and things can get back to normal." We had been on a horrific journey, and we were aware that we weren't exactly at the finish line, but we were looking for a place to sit down and rest from the journey just for awhile. I quickly realized that I wasn't going to find that place of rest yet. I realized that Bob didn't need one hundred percent of my attention any longer and decided to divert part of my mind to work again. The first week there I just sat at my desk and asked Paula what I should do. She tasked me. She also cried everyday for the first week.

I kept telling her, "Don't cry! It's okay! Bob's going to get better; the business is still here…a little beat up…but nevertheless, still here. We're going to be fine."

She continued to cry and say, "You don't know. You just don't understand."

It quickly dawned on me. I began to understand. Our business (God's business) was still there but really just barely. We had lost over half of our crew, and it was apparent that everyone was in crisis mode. The battlefield of my life had spilled over into my business. Everyone who worked for us was just realizing that. The battle of business was continuing to be waged everyday, but there was no real battle plan here. There were no generals. Everyone was on autopilot. There were no leaders casting visions, only workers doing what they knew how to do on their own. The management staff that we had were all very close to Bob and me and had obviously been emotionally suffering the loss. They were not prepared to take over the business; they were not prepared to lead. They did an awesome job of keeping the ship afloat, and I am forever thankful for the dedication and loyalty that was shown over that period of time, but I believe Paula was the only one who truly realized that financially the ship was sinking and fast.

My dad had assumed a role of shop manager and was there at least ten hours everyday. He was also keenly aware that things were not operating at one hundred percent. John was our senior superintendent and assumed the role of operating manager over the period of time that we were gone. He worked with the passion and dedication of a business owner but lacked the knowledge of many essential details of the newly acquired position that could have helped him to be more comfortable in his new role. Someone later referred to John's new role within the company as a "battlefield promotion." How true that statement was.

As I dug myself back into work, I began to realize the sheer exhaustion under which I was operating. I couldn't concentrate on digging us out of the hole that we'd fallen into because I was too busy with helping to put out the fires that kept vying for my immediate attention. One project in particular was vying for immediate action. A customer called and stated that our jobsite crew was not performing well on a project that we had contracted to complete. He then told me that our crew was also refusing to perform part of our contracted work.

He then described a task that needed to be performed on the jobsite that would be an approximate five thousand dollar cost to us. It was work that was not in our contract and not in our written estimate to perform. I explained this to him and told him that we would be happy to perform the work at an additional cost. He became belligerent with me. He told me that his company had Bob's verbal promise that he would do this work. I asked how Bob could promise to do something four months ago that no one knew existed until just recently. He wanted to speak to Bob. I told him that Bob was on a medical leave of absence and had almost lost his life. He told me that he was sorry that Bob was sick, but that Bob had promised to do the work just recently. I told him that there was no way that Bob could have spoken to him recently. This resulted in more belligerence and then a bold-faced lie. He told me that he had Bob on tape promising this work. He told me to schedule the crew to perform the work, and he'd have the tape pulled out of archives and have it mailed to us. I believe that they took Bob's condition as an excuse to cheat our company out of five thousand dollars worth of work. I had to fly my brother Rusty in to Denver to help with that project. It seemed that no one else in our company could stand up to the monster on the jobsite. We eventually finished. We lost three more employees on that job.

March 4, 2004:

God, I speak to You because You are a safe place. I don't know how to do this anymore. Help me, God. Give me peace. Today Roger resigned at work. Three months ago he shaved his head in support of Bob undergoing chemotherapy; now he's gone. He's scared. Help me again, Lord. Thank you for being there. SCI is Yours, always has been, always will be.

March 6, 2004:

It's Saturday. Bob's been home for one week and two days now. I'm so tired; it's like two full-time jobs! I sleep lightly next to him, listening for his breathing, and hearing the tube-feeding machine whirring. I assist him to the bathroom twice a night and thank You, God, that he's not incontinent in the bed. Then I am up at 6:30 A.M. to discontinue the tube feedings, give morning medications through the J-tube, and get ready for work. I have to help Bob downstairs and into the shower. He sits on the shower chair and washes himself now. Mom comes over and I "pass off" the patient to her. Work is so heavy on me. I don't want to be there, but can't stay away.

Bob sees the nurse two times per week, P.T., and speech therapy, too. At least two doctor visits per week: Mom takes him to a few for me, so I can work. I get home from work at 6 P.M., and Mom is giving me the report as I walk in the door. I hardly have time to put my purse down, and she's telling me, "I didn't give him his 6 P.M. meds yet, thought I'd wait for you. Started his tube feeding at four, he had a good day. Vital signs are in the book, no fevers, and the bedsore looks better…" I feel like crying. Stop!! I need a minute first. I can't continue at this pace, I really can't.

31
Finish the Race

March of 2004 continued the same. I worked too many hours trying to fix things that I really didn't care about. I spent time at home with Bob as his nurse and not his wife. Bob gained his strength and his voice back very slowly. The physical therapist stopped seeing him because he was progressing on his own. The speech therapist continued twice per week and brought word searches, crossword books, and homework for Bob to do. I helped as much as possible, but sometimes coming home in the evening, I just wanted to be a wife again.

One evening in March, Bob accidentally pulled his J-tube out of his stomach. We scheduled a test the next morning at the hospital to see if he would have to have it reinserted or if he'd be able to start eating on his own. He passed the test, and Bob finally was started on a real diet! We went straight from the hospital to a restaurant, and he ordered french-fries and a chocolate shake. He ate only one french-fry and half of the shake. I was happy that Bob could eat again, but I began to feel sorry for myself because this just meant that now I would have to add "cook" to my resume.

March 21, 2004:

Battle rages on. Different now, but still there. Work, disease, too busy? Too much? Am I being too selfish? I need to stop thinking about myself. Work is not going well. I don't want to keep fighting it. I don't know if I can. God, please give us the patience and the character to wait for this manifestation of healing. Healing is ours; healing is ours.

One day, late in March, we received a message from the cancer center. Bob's doctors had been drawing blood with every visit, and the blood test results were back. So was the cancer.

Dr. Jeffries scheduled Bob for chemotherapy again on April 6, Passover. We took communion together and prayed before we went to the cancer center. We prayed that the blood of the Lamb was on us, on the doorpost, and the angel of death would see the blood and pass over us, too. No more death.

I asked God, "Am I losing it all because I wasn't thankful for what I had been blessed with? God, forgive me." But then just as quickly I would answer myself, "No, no, no! This is not a punishment from God. This is not our fault. This is just what it is. A disease, an enemy who is trying to steal the life that God had given us." We couldn't let it.

Chemo went very well. It was quite uneventful, just as the first dose had been. This time the doctors were overly precautious and scheduled Bob to come in every week for blood work and for injections to help build his white and red blood cells.

Bob continued to increase in physical strength during April despite the chemotherapy. He decided that he wanted to go back to work. I let him. He sat at his desk; I cried to see him there. He tried so hard to actually work. I think it was therapeutic for him to be there, to hear the work going on around him, to see it. He told me repeatedly that he was sorry that work was so hard on me. I tried not to let him see how it wore on me, but, unfortunately, I wasn't very good at hiding it.

On April 20th, we were called by a customer who wanted to award us the largest contract our company had ever had. It was a project that Bob had estimated before he became sick. He was the only one who knew details of the project. I was petrified. Here I was trying to decide whether or not to shut the doors, to quit for awhile, to take a break, and we were being offered a project that would most likely last close to a year. I knew that the decision that I was about to make wasn't just "Do we take the job?" It was, "Do we stay open?" I wasn't ready to make that decision, yet I would have to. Under the pressure of making the decision, I began to crack.

I prayed, and then waited for the answer. I still felt like I was going crazy. I made lists of reasons to close the business and reasons to keep it open. Every reason to close was motivated by fear and doubt. I knew that those were the wrong reasons. I waited as long as I could for God to tell me to quit; I gave Him every chance. He never did. He told me to finish the race. He told me to run the race with perseverance.

2 Timothy 4:7 I have fought the good fight, I have finished the race, I have kept the faith. (NIV Bible)

I felt like my faith was just a spark, a small flickering spark. I was so worn out, so tired. Even a spark chases away darkness. My faith began to grow again. The spark became a fire. I would endure by His Spirit, not by my power. He had kept us so far; He would keep us until the end. I began the familiar fight. I spoke to myself aloud every day concerning work.

"I still believe. Thank You, God, I will endure. Strengthen me. We will survive this, too."

While I was decided that we would survive, five more of our long-time crew members evidently feared that we wouldn't. In one week all five quit. We were down to a skeleton crew.

This fight felt as hard as the one for Bob's life. Every time I began to grow in faith, another hit came from the enemy.

Rusty called one morning and said, "Keep your left up."

I would. My left hand held the shield, the shield of faith. My right hand held God's hand.

Isaiah 41:13 For I am the Lord, your God, who takes hold of your right hand and says to you, do not fear; I will help you. (NIV Bible)

April 2004:

I surrender; none of it is mine. None of it. Help me to walk the walk with no fear. By Your spirit, God, give me what I need. You know how scared I am, God. You know that I'm leaning on You. I'll believe that You are in control of my surrendered life. Shut up, Satan! You are a liar. You are the loser; I win in God. He's my deliverer. I have been to the camp of the enemy; I've been there. Thank you, Hope. The spoils are His to do with what He pleases. I don't have a big problem, I have a big God.

I had decided that we would take the contract, we would do the work and that God would provide. I concluded that if our business was indeed God's business, and if He felt that He wanted to bless us with this very large contract in the midst of Bob's battle with death, so be it. God would provide the manpower and the strength for us to do so.

Bob's doctor visits and chemotherapy treatments still occupied at least two days per week in April. I continued to try and hold myself and our company together while taking him to his clinic visits. It was like living two different lives, the one we were trying to get away from and the one we were trying to get back to.

In early May, the customer who had awarded us the large project called. They wanted us to come to a meeting and go over the details of the contract and sign it. Bob wanted to go to the meeting. One of the worst feelings that I had during this time was the guilt that I felt when telling Bob that he couldn't meet with people at work. He wanted to meet customers and work as usual. I tried to keep him away from our customers for fear that they would take one look at him and decide to go with another demolition contractor. He was a fearful sight. Although we all told him how great he looked, it was because we had seen him worse. The public had not, and to the public, he looked scary. This fact was brought to my attention frequently.

One day at the pharmacy, waiting for Bob's medication, the technician asked if I wanted to sign for my grandfather's medication, so when Bob wanted to go to the meeting with our newest and largest customer, I hesitated, but decided that I needed him there. He knew more about the project than anyone else, and he would just have to step up to the plate. John, Bob, and I attended. John and I did most of the talking and confidently assured the customer that we would perform the project. We discussed a few details. Bob spoke briefly but succinctly.

The customer slid the contract across the table to me, handed me a pen and said, "Well, I guess all that's left is for us to sign."

Could anyone else hear my heart beating?

I prayed as I signed my name, "God, You are our provision; I accept what You have to give us."

We had just signed a contract for the largest project that we had ever taken in the nine year history of our company, and Bob's only statement upon leaving the jobsite trailer was, "I'm glad I wore a diaper, because I don't think I'm gonna be able to hold it until we get back to the office."

We readied ourselves for the work. We hired fifteen people, and I contracted subcontractors to help. John and Paula were excited to have work to concentrate on again. I was happy that we would have income to pay our bills. God was going to provide. I learned very early on in my relationship with God that giving was the key to receiving. We tithed off of our income faithfully, and God was faithful to provide more than we needed in return. During this time of instability in our business, we watched our income dry up. I knew that God still provided; I knew that I still had to plant seed in order to reap a harvest. Though our company was into a credit line to the tune of nearly $100,000, and Bob and I had sold one of our rental houses to pay our own personal bills, I still planted financial seed. I had already learned this lesson from God, and I wasn't about to turn my back on what I knew was true. I sacrificially gave of our finances during this time. Our income had been cut in half, yet we gave three times as much as we had the previous year. I was believing God to provide healing in Bob and in our business, and I wanted Him to know that I trusted Him.

32
Going to Transplant

The second week in May we visited the cancer center for Bob's weekly "red blood cell boosting" injection. The BMT Coordinator wanted to speak to us.

What now?

"Bob and Kim, I have great news."

It was about time. "Bob, your last blood test shows that the chemo is working, and the cancer markers are normal."

Before she even let that wonderful good news sink in she hit us with, "We think you're strong enough, so let's go to transplant!"

Evidently the look of fear and panic on my face was a shock to her. "This is good news!" She encouraged us.

I wasn't ready. Bob was. "Bring it on!" He said, "Let's go for it." I began to get a sick feeling in the pit of my stomach and thought I might vomit. That feeling lasted the entire time she explained our upcoming schedule of events and the entire drive home. I called and informed both of our families and tried to be brave and encouraging to them as they asked the questions that I had been asking myself. "Is he strong enough? Aren't his kidneys still a concern? Has he put on enough weight? Can't they give us a little more time?" I explained that Bob was ready and that this was what we had been waiting for, so it was time.

We started the re-staging tests at the hospital and signed the consents for the transplant. The doctors were excited and told us that after what had happened to Bob, they didn't think he would have ever made it to this stage of treatment. I had hoped that after everything we'd gone through, God would have completely healed him of the cancer, but I shut up and carried my cross.

I tried to continue work during May, knowing that I would probably be in the hospital with Bob for the month of his transplant. Employees still wanted their evaluations and raises. I still needed to send contract documents and billing forms to customers. Our estimators and our newly-hired project manager still needed to be managed. Taxes still had to be paid. My mom said once that no matter what happens in life, life still goes on.

When her mother died, she remembered seeing the sink full of dishes and thinking to herself, "My mother just died, and I still have to do the dishes."

I knew the feeling. Bob and I were getting ready to go back to the battlefield and face cancer and death, and I had to "do the dishes" first. I put off as many of those "dishes" as I could. I paid the bills, opened the mail, and prioritized what needed to be addressed immediately. I tried to keep tabs on my two teenage daughters who were getting lost in the shuffle of it all, but I could not and would not take on anything that was not emergent. The letter I opened from the IRS stating that they were trying to gather information regarding our tax returns from two years earlier in order to audit them was one that I considered emergent.

I called our accountant and said, "Paul, I have a letter from the IRS, and it looks like they need some information on past years' taxes. Can you help with this?"

He told me to fax the letter over, and he'd see what he could do. I quickly dismissed it. A few hours later, Paul called back and told me that I would need to gather some documents from our 2002 income tax return and mail it to him, and he would forward it to the IRS for the audit.

I told Paul, "I don't have time for an audit right now!" He assured me that he would help. The only information the IRS wound up wanting was proof of the charitable giving that we had paid. We mailed copies of the tithing receipts from our church, and they were satisfied. I still can't believe that in the midst of everything that was happening, we were audited.

From May 25-June 4, we reported to the outpatient center for stem cell collection. Bob had reached 10.7 million cells. We were going to have a break for a week or two then be admitted for transplant. Bob said that I cried in my sleep. He didn't want to wake me. I don't remember my dreams. I know that I tried to be so strong while I was awake. Maybe the only time I truly relaxed was while I slept, and when I let my guard down, I cried.

33
Failed Transplant: I Hate Losing

The entire month of transplant, we lived by a calendar. I remember making these calendars for my bone marrow transplant patients. Chemotherapy starts on Day -2. Day 0 is the day of receiving stem cells back. It's like a new start, a new birth. Day zero. Rescue and rebuilding starts after day zero.

Day zero was June 16, 2004. My mother, Hope, Kathy, and I were with Bob during his stem cell transfusion. It went very well, very smoothly. The transplant almost seemed anticlimactic.

We fell back into our old routine. Praise and worship music played in his room, the prayer shawl hung over the footboard of his bed. Cards, pictures, and posters were hung on the walls. The only difference was that Bob was awake, talking, and eating. The nurses and staff didn't recognize him. They all laughed at the difference in him.

"Bob, you don't even know us!" they would say to him.

"No, sorry," he would respond. Therapists and doctors would come to visit just to see how wonderful he looked. The most wonderful part of this hospitalization was that I could speak to Bob from home. Upon arriving home at night, I would call him to say good night. He would call me in the morning to wake me. This time was different. I didn't fear leaving him.

One night he called me back after I had fallen asleep, "Kim, I'm sorry. Did I wake you?"

"It's okay, what's wrong?" I sat up, heart pounding, scared again.

He began to cry. "I'm reading this book about healing. Kim, I get it! Jesus came here to earth to heal us!" It was so simple. So very simple.

Talk about revelation moments. I began to cry with him.

"Yes, Bob! You're right."

"He WANTS to heal me!" He was ecstatic. I laughed out loud.

Thank You, God.

By day seven, Bob was receiving platelet and blood transfusions regularly. His blood cells had died, the new marrow hadn't kicked in yet, and he was needing the transfusions to hold him over until the new stem cells engrafted into his bone marrow and started producing cells. Normal course, he was still doing very well. His family and mine donated blood and platelets for him every few days. During this week we heard the news that Paula's life-long friend Nancy, who was battling cancer, was not doing well and was given only two months to live. I was so confused. It seemed like death was all around. We were just trying to get out alive.

By the second week, Bob was starting to get more symptoms from the chemo, and his blood counts were still low, no engraftment yet. He started to develop mouth sores, throat pain severe enough for him to need I.V. narcotics, and horrible diarrhea.

On day nine, he spiked a fever of 100.3. I lost it. One of the nurses who had cared for Bob during the last hospital stay, grabbed me by the arms, and looked me square in the face.

"It's going to be okay. They all get fevers. It's going to be okay."

"But his white count is too low!" I was fearing a repeat of the last stay.

"Kim, he's going to be okay." She was very calm.

Day fifteen. Nancy died.

July 1, 2004:

Nancy died. She's in heaven. Why do some die and some live? Why are we still here? Why Bob? Why Nancy? Nancy told Paula she saw angels. I've seen them too. She wasn't afraid. Paula spent time with her, prayed with her before she left. I'm not afraid.

By Day 16, we were only waiting for the diarrhea to subside in order to be discharged.

On July 3rd, Bob came home. He was very tired and not keeping much food down. Normal course. It was time to gain strength. He was healed.

On July 15th, Dr. Jeffries decided that it was time to draw the Light Chain test again. We were drawing cancer markers. I was so excited; this was it! We were going to see that Bob had been healed once and for all.

On July 22nd, we entered the treatment room at the cancer center. The nurses wouldn't look us in the eyes. No one seemed to notice us. Dr. Jeffries was sitting behind the desk and wouldn't look up when we came in. Something was wrong.

"Put Bob in a room," he quietly said to his nurse.

"Hi, Bob. Can you come over here? We're going to put you in a room today," she said, trying to sound cheerful. They hadn't taken his vital signs or drawn blood. They were out of their routine; something was definitely wrong. We walked into the private room, and he sat on the bed. I paced back and forth.

"Something's wrong," I said aloud.

"What?!" Bob had not picked up on any of it. "How do you know? What's wrong?" He was picking up on my fear.

"Shhh!" I wanted him to be quiet because I was listening to them talk at the desk. I barely made out Dr. Jeffries saying "Light Chains… (something I couldn't make out)… damn it!" Oh, God! This was bad. He entered the room and shut the door behind him. "Hi, Bob," he said as if he were apologizing.

No! I didn't want to hear this. No! I had seen this before. I had sat on the other side of this before. No! I didn't want to do this!

He placed his hand on Bob's shoulder. "Bob." It seemed to be in slow motion. "I'm sorry." No! Don't be sorry! No! "The Light Chain test came back, and the cancer is still there. It looks like the transplant didn't work. I'm so sorry, Bob."

He kept his hand on Bob's shoulder. Bob looked like a child, so confused. "What?" Silence.

"I'm sorry, Bob. We'll draw the test again just to make sure, but it came back at sixty-five, it should be normal after transplant."

He looked at me. "Kim?"

Before I could realize what I was saying, I heard myself yell, "NO! NO! NO!" I started to cry in anger, "Do you know what we've been through!?" Then, realizing whom I was talking to, "Of course you do! You were there. Do you know that it's been a year now?! We've been fighting this for a year! Why?" I began to cry.

Bob started to cry.

"We're not going to give up," Dr. Jeffries tried to console us. Time seemed to stop. It seemed as we sat there silently, he was watching us to make sure that we had comprehended this horrible news. "We've got other things we can try. I'm sorry, Bob. I'm going to have the nurses draw the test again, just to make sure. Then you can go over to the hospital and have that pheresis catheter removed today. You won't need any more blood products. I think it's time to take it out. Let's make an appointment for next week; we'll discuss where to go from here. I'm so sorry, you guys. Let me know if you need anything at all."

With that, he got up and left. He held his head down as he walked out of the room. I sat next to Bob on the bed and held him. We cried together until the nurse came in and drew the cancer marker again. We then got up and walked over to the hospital that was across the street to have the catheter pulled. We walked like zombies. We held hands but didn't talk to each other. What was there to say?

We signed in at the radiology desk. We'd been there before. It was so familiar. The T. V. in the waiting room was too loud. *The Montel Williams Show* was on. Why was everyone so interested in someone else's dirty laundry? I didn't want to listen to it. Bob and I sat silently. I was too upset to cry. I was too exhausted to talk. I felt like the wind had been knocked out of me.

"Bob Hritz," the man in scrubs came in and called Bob back for the procedure. "He'll only be a few minutes." He smiled at me. He didn't have any idea what we'd just been told. I looked around the waiting room at the people who were watching Montel question this young girl about her cheating boyfriend; they didn't know either. I was sitting there among all of those people, yet was all alone. Oh, God, why have You forsaken me? Where are You in all of this?

What did I fight so hard for? To lose it all? Is it coming to pass? Am I losing it all? It sure felt like it.

****

The words "failed transplant" kept repeating in my head. I couldn't stop it. Failed transplant, failed transplant, failed transplant. This was bad. I knew it. I remember taking care of patients who had failed transplant. There wasn't much more to do. Oh, I'm sure that the doctors would look through their book of tricks… experimental drugs, study drugs, clinical trials. I was so tired of the fight. I couldn't even allow my thoughts to wander to what would be next. They finished pulling Bob's catheter, and we walked out to the car.

Once behind the wheel of the car, I broke the silence, "I'm so sorry, Bob." I didn't have any tears to cry, I honestly didn't have the energy to. What he said blessed me, revived me.

"I'm not giving up on God!" He sounded angry. Angry at cancer? I didn't ask. That was the extent of our conversation. We drove home in silence. I couldn't help but feel like we were being beat, like we were losing the fight. I hated losing.

July 24, 2004:

Thursday's doctor visit didn't give us the verbalization from the doctor that we wanted. He says that Bob's Light Chains are sixty-five. That's up from last time, up from before transplant. He grew through transplant. This is not normal. They should be under twenty. Maybe this is where God wants us. It's just a reminder of the disease that Bob has been healed of.

I'm so tired. Whom can I tell? Whom can I tell that I'm tired? I miss Bob so much it feels like I could throw up. He hasn't even made it back to full strength yet, he hasn't even come back fully and now this? I wonder if this is what it feels like to those who have lost a loved one: change, sorrow, self-pity, loneliness. What do they feel that I don't? What does it matter? Grief,sorrow. That's all. Sometimes, God, I wonder if it would have been easier if he would have died. I'm sorry, Father, forgive me, but I wonder. I am so tired, God, so very tired.

I don't know what to do anymore. I haven't a clue.

July 25, 2004

We went to church and a pastor stood up and said, "I have a word for some of you. I speak to all of you who are tired, all who are weary, who are laid low. God says to you: FIND YOUR REST IN ME. Come to me, all who are weary and heavy laden. Seek me. You are tired because you are trying to do this all in your own power. Rest in me. I will give you power, strength. Yoke with me."

WOW!!!!

Bob and I would rest in Him.

The next week Bob and I went to see a dermatologist. It was an appointment that we'd made the previous week to diagnose what was causing a newly-developed skin rash. Upon entering her exam room, she stated very matter-of-factly, "I've read your history, and my concern is that this rash is a presentation of the myeloma. I'm going to do a biopsy, and it will take at least a week for us to get the results back. Until then, if you're not uncomfortable…?"

Was that a question? Was she actually wanting us to answer? Bob shook his head, indicating that he wasn't uncomfortable.

She continued, "Then we will just wait for the results. I'll call you as soon as I get them." Okay. Another hit.

Tuesday of that week, Dr. Jeffries office called. The new Light Chain test was back, and it was now sixty-nine. There was no mistake: Bob had failed transplant. It was sinking in. Another hit.

The enemy was throwing everything he had at us. Did he know we were down? Did he think we were against the ropes, tired, down and out, and he thought to deliver the finishing blow? From somewhere, Bob and I found strength. In our surrendered, beaten, defeated state, God rose up yet again. In our weakness, He truly was made strong. Nothing else mattered, but that He was strong. He was God. He would be the finisher of this thing. He would be the end of this fight.

34
It is Finished

Doctor's visits continued. The BMT doctor wanted to start Bob on a new drug that was still being studied for myeloma. The infectious disease doctor wanted to keep seeing Bob every two weeks to assess the nocardia infection and his continued need for antibiotics. The nephrologist wanted to continue seeing Bob weekly for kidney function tests. The neurologist still wanted to follow the encephalitis with MRI's and EEG's. Bob and I bowed out. We refused the invitation to continue the dance. We surrendered our dance shoes. At approximately the same time, the same week, Bob and I both decided that we didn't want to see the doctors anymore. We didn't want to try the new treatments, didn't want to take the drugs anymore. We really were finished.

When I first felt this, I asked Paula, "Do you think I should tell Bob? I'm really feeling like we should stop now. God keeps telling me to stop, but I want him to make his own decision."

Paula said, "Pray for confirmation."

I did. I prayed that if God were telling me to stop, that he would tell Bob the same thing. I prayed that God would tell the doctors to stop, too. I prayed for each and every one of Bob's doctors. "God, let them hear Your voice, give them wisdom that comes from You." Our next visit at the cancer center was approaching. I asked Bob, "What are you going to do?"

He replied the confirmation that I had asked of God. "Kim, I keep praying, and all I keep getting is 'Do nothing'." He was confused.

I hugged him and cried. "That's what I get, too. I think it's time to stop. Let's be still, and know that He is God."

August 5th was my thirty-ninth birthday. It was also our next appointment with Dr. Jeffries at the cancer center.

We met with Dr. Jeffries at 11:00 A. M. I silently prayed as he walked into the room. "God, please don't let this be a fight."

"How are you feeling, Bob?" He was cheerful.

"Great!" Bob was starting to speak in faith.

"Well, I've been looking into this new drug, and it is showing great results in the treatment of myeloma, so I would assume that KLCDD would show the same results. We could put a port-a-cath I.V. line in your chest. It would sit under the skin, so you wouldn't have to worry about showering or anything. We can give you the drug through it and draw blood through it, too. The treatments only last about ten minutes. You'll be in and out of here in no time."

"We've decided that we don't want to do anything more," Bob spoke as if he hadn't heard a word the doctor had said. I continued to pray silently.

"Okay, Bob, I understand that it's been a rough year for you." He seemed to be getting it.

"We really just don't want to have anymore treatment," I interrupted. "What other drugs can he stop taking? It's time for him to stop taking all these drugs." Where was this coming from? I was so bold.

Dr. Jeffries closed Bob's chart and put his hand up to his chin. He sighed, "I'll tell you what. I'm going to give you a break. I'm going to give you six weeks off. You need the time off." He opened the chart again and looked through the medication list. "The only thing that I prescribed is Prilosec and the Coumadin for the filter. If you don't have a problem with the heartburn, you can stop the Prilosec, but you can't go off the blood thinner due to the filter." Good enough. We were happy. No chemo and one pill gone.

We were on such a roll, we called the infectious disease doctor that afternoon and told him that we wanted to stop the antibiotics. He told us to come in and see him first. We made an appointment and told him the same thing face to face. "We want to be off of every drug that we can get off of."

"Any fevers?" he asked as he poked on Bob's belly. "Any chills?" No to both.

"We don't want to keep seeing so many doctors and taking so many pills We're finished." Bob was bold, too.

He stood still and looked at us for a full minute.

"That infection I had was pretty bad, huh?" Bob broke the silence.

"Yes, one of the worst I've seen," he replied. It sounded like Bob was starting to forget his mission to get off drugs.

"Well, God healed me from that, so he'll take care of me now." Nope, still on.

"Well, that may be your bias, but I believe the antibiotics saved you.

"Okay, you can stop the antibiotics, but if you get any fevers, you need to call me immediately, okay?"

The next doctor that we "faced off with" was the nephrologist. "We don't want to be on drugs anymore; what can he stop taking?" I must have sounded angry because his answer surprised me.

"Are you mad at the doctors, Kim?"

"No Dr. Richards I'm not mad at you or any of the doctors, but I'm mad as hell at cancer and death. We're not going to bow down to them anymore. We're finished. We are people of faith, believing God for a miracle, and it's hard to walk in that faith when we see doctors every week and take hands full of pills every day."

"Okay," he replied. He opened the chart and told us to cut back on the anti-diuretics that helped Bob to urinate. He said he'd try to wean him off of the blood pressure pills as well but that might be a slower process. He didn't want his kidneys to be damaged anymore by something that could be controlled with medication. He also ordered another twenty-four hour urine collection. He wanted to get a better test on exactly how well Bob's kidneys were operating.

Bob told him, "They'll be at 100%."

Dr. Richards said, "That would be something, Bob, but I doubt it." We didn't doubt.

The dermatologist called and left a message on our answering machine. "Just wanting to give you results, I'll call Dr. Jeffries at the cancer center." Bob and I erased the message and decided not to call back. We didn't care one way or the other.

The final doctor to see was the neurologist. He was the doctor to whom the other doctors attributed saving Bob's life. He had diagnosed the encephalitis and started the drugs that eventually helped Bob to wake up in the hospital back in February. Bob wanted to drive to the doctor's office. It was the first time he would drive in eight months. I let him.

"Please don't kill me!" I joked.

"I'll be careful," he said.

This visit was by far the best doctor's visit we had ever, and to this day, have ever had. Dr. Trevor came to the waiting room himself to get us. He hugged Bob and I and told us how happy he was to see us.

"Oh, my gosh! You look great!" He was honestly excited to see us.

"I drove here." Bob was so proud.

"Get outta here!" he joked back. "Who would have ever thought!?"

We sat in the exam room and started with our mantra, "We're sick of being sick and would like to be taken off of every drug possible. We're acting in faith by saying Bob is healed and then at the same time taking too many pills and seeing too many doctors..."

"Okay, I understand," he interrupted. "You know we're not God. We do the best we can, but God has to step in."

Whoa! He was on our side!

He described the temporal lobe's role in personality and depression and seizure activity. He talked science and faith. This was unusual. He told us that Bob could cut his seizure medication from three times a day to two times per day and that he'd eventually wean him completely. He told him to schedule his next MRI for three months and that he wouldn't even need to see us for six months. Then he told us a story.

"Bob and Kim, I have to tell you something." He closed the chart, pushed his rolling stool back against the wall, leaned back, and crossed his legs. "Bob, you are amazing. It is a miracle that you are alive, let alone talking and driving. I look at your MRI and say, 'This man is a vegetable,' then I see you... wow." We all smiled.

"I was raised Catholic, but when I went to medical school, I started to question God because I started believing more in science than in God. You know, it's hard to go through medical school and not doubt God. So anyway, then

I see patients all the time who are so sick and don't get better... Not long ago, I started asking God, praying, I guess. 'God, if you are really there...'" He didn't finish that sentence. His voice started to crack a bit.

"So one night last January, I'm on call at the hospital, and I get called about a guy who's having seizures in the ER, and I eventually meet you two. Well, I don't know if you know this, but I was really new to the hospital, and your case had so many doctors consulting: infectious disease, nephrology, bone marrow transplant, the medical team, and me. So, I'm the new kid on the block, you know? After looking at your MRI's and examining you and then hearing the other doctors' opinions about strokes and blood clots, it just didn't add up to me. You know how you get this feeling in your gut; you can't explain it, but it is there and so strong? I kept saying, 'It's not a stroke, something about this isn't right.'"

I understood what he was saying; it was wisdom. I nodded my head and replied, "I know what you are saying."

"So anyway, you know that it wasn't a clot, and I'm glad that I followed that gut feeling. More importantly, I felt like God had answered my prayer. I watched the faith that you and your family had in this whole thing and..." He shook his head and choked up a bit. "...I even called my mom and told her about what had happened. I told her about the faith that you guys had. I told her, 'Bob is a miracle'." A tear rolled down his cheek. He wiped it away and looked at Bob, "Bob, you shouldn't be alive right now! I don't know if you understand. You are a miracle!"

We understood. We knew. Bob cried. All I could say was, "God is so cool. Look how many people He has touched in this."

Dr. Trevor agreed, "Yes, God IS cool." He hugged us goodbye and told us that he'd see us in six months.

We had divorced ourselves from weekly doctor visits, weekly blood draws, and hands full of pills. We were surrendered totally to God.

We were free.

35
Victory in Christ

Freedom from the health care routine didn't actually mean freedom from our thoughts. The six weeks that we had taken off were surprisingly hard.

Bob and I decided to attend one of our church's cell group meetings. Hope recommended one of these groups to us, told us that we should go. On August 8th, we attended a cell group meeting. We tried quietly to blend in, but a woman seated across from us asked if Bob were okay. I was so used to seeing him that I had forgotten how sick he must look to everyone else. "Yes, he just had a bone marrow transplant," I replied casually.

"Do you need us to pray for you?" She looked at Bob. He nodded.

Deborah, one of the group leaders, came to me and grabbed me by the arm. "You've been in a battle," she said it very matter-of-factly, very knowingly. I stared into her eyes. How did she know? Did I wear it physically as much as spiritually, or was she reading me spiritually? It didn't matter; she knew. We stared at each other.

I nodded my head, "You bet I have." She hugged me and told Bob and me to sit down in the middle of the room. They were going to lay hands on us and pray for us. Someone asked us to share with the group what had happened. Were they ready for this? Were we? I gave the two-minute story (I was getting used to that one), and they all stared at Bob as I talked.

"…so we aren't seeing doctors anymore, we are going to leave this in God's hands now. We're going to keep believing Him and only Him for total healing." I ended my two minutes.

Deborah took over. She spoke with authority. Others in the group came toward us. The all laid their hands on the both of us and began to pray. I was overwhelmed with the love and support that these complete strangers were giving us. I broke down and cried. Bob started to share with them, through his broken speech, that he had been prideful, that he thought that he was such a tough guy, and now he knew that God was the tough one. He repented of his pride, asked God to forgive him. He truly repented in this room full of strangers, of something that he had never admitted to anyone else. He was confessing to God and to man. He was asking God's forgiveness.

I don't even remember what they prayed; I just felt their love, and it overwhelmed me. I do remember that someone asked Bob if he had been filled with the Holy Spirit, if he spoke in tongues.

"No, I've tried; I've asked God to help me, but no."

They began to pray for him to be filled with the Holy Spirit. Bob began to pray in tongues next to me. I heard him; he wept as he prayed. Wow, I was more overwhelmed. I had cried more in that room with those strangers than I had in front of my family. It was more surrendering. The meeting ended, Bob and I finished the box of Kleenex that sat on the table, thanked everyone, and left.

Jon and Eileen, who had hosted the meeting, hugged us goodbye and told us to come back soon. They told us that they would keep praying for us and would keep believing with us. We thanked them and told them we'd definitely be back. As we sat in Bob's truck in front of their house, Bob broke down and cried again. "Kim, nothing like that has ever happened to me before." I couldn't help but laugh. It seemed so inappropriate, but I couldn't stop. He continued through his sobs, "When they touched me, I felt heat, like electricity, running all through my body. I felt it all through me. It came out my toes. I still feel it in my toes! God just touched me!" Boy, had He. We stayed in front of the house, in the cab of the truck until he stopped crying. My laughter continued.

It felt so good to laugh that I didn't want to stop.

* * * * * * *

The freedom came in bouts. I was surrendered to God but still fought with what that meant. Did that mean that we were giving up, and Bob would die? Did it mean he would finally be totally healed? I didn't know. I only knew that God had taken over, and that whatever happened, was His will. I would survive it, whatever it was. For the most part, Bob and I lived day-by-day. Work continued to be stressful, the dishes continued to fill the sink, and the bills continued to pile up. We just lived.

August 13, 2004:

Feeling sorry for myself again. I'll be okay, it's only when I think of me and Bob and how hard this has been on us that I get sad. Selfish. Faith, Kim, faith. Why, God? Why is this happening? Will I ever know? Do I really care? I love You, God; I know You know what's best. It's so hard. I lean on You, God. Don't let me fall. I'm hanging by a thread.

Bob woke in the middle of the night last night and vomited. I was only half-awake, but it brought a flood of emotions and memories. I jumped up and grabbed a cold cloth for him. When he fell back asleep, I had a horrible dream, "He's still sick! What makes you think he's okay? Why do you think he's healed? Look at him!" Bob says I cried in my sleep again. *Wow, the enemy is relentless. He just doesn't stop. Flee! Cancer doesn't live her anymore. Period.*

On August 16th, Bob's blood pressure started rising. Fear was fighting the good fight too. Bob and I took a step of faith and ignored the blood pressure, ignored the fear, and took Katie to the car dealer and bought her the car we had promised her before this whole mess had started. Faith.

Bob also decided that he wasn't going to sit around and wait for something to happen. He was going to start making things happen. He had been reading his Bible every morning and was filling himself up with faith. He said, "I'm going to call my soccer team and see if they can play me."

I was a little nervous, but I decided that it was better than sitting and waiting for another symptom to show itself. "Why not?" I told him. "Live!"

What an awesome sight to see those white, skinny atrophied legs in soccer shorts. With his uniform and pads on, he actually started to look like he might be able to play. His team was awesome. They were so happy to see him; they let him play goalie for a period. It scared the crap out of me to see the other team charging toward him with the ball.

I wanted to scream, "He's on Coumadin! Don't kick him!" I restrained myself. He was absolutely horrible. His reflexes were slow, he didn't have the energy to run, but he loved every minute of it.

"I suck!" he stated to his teammates after the game. They didn't care about the game, the loss. They let him play.

"Bobby, you rock! You were awesome! We can't believe you even came out tonight."

They are such an amazing group of guys. Bob showed them his scars and told them his story. They were amazed. So was I. He was living; he was going to suck every breath out of life as long as he could.

By September, Bob had been working a few days a week. He was not back fully yet, physically or mentally, but he was trying so hard. He was showing so much faith by being there. It was easier for me to be there when I looked in and saw him at his desk.

September 1, 2004:

How do I walk this walk every day? It feels like a tight rope like a balancing act between God and life. I've wanted to get back into this safe place, that cleft in the rock. I haven't been there since God placed me there in January. Now my walk is different; I can't just hide from life. I have to live it. This is what we asked for though, isn't it? Life. Live more abundantly. Bob is alive. He walks, talks, works, drives, eats, laughs, and prays. I thank God. I thank You, God. Praise God for the miracle of life. Life is now down to two times a day of taking pills. Bob takes them himself without my help. He's starting to get hair again. It's very fuzzy. He wakes up in the morning and gets ready for work by himself. He leaves the house with a change of clothes and a diaper. We sit at work all day and put out the fires.

God is faithful. In the valley, He is there, and on the mountaintop, He is there. He is faithful. In the midst of the storm, He is there, and when the sun shines, He is there. He is faithful. On the front lines of the battle, He is there. When I lay down my sword, He picks it up and fights for me. He is faithful.

We must have been so stubborn. It took us so long to completely surrender in every area. I remember being in church, and during praise and worship, I would always catch myself with my hands in fists.

"Why?" I asked God. "Why am I fighting during worship?"

"You are a warrior."

"I don't want to fight You, though, God."

"So don't."

Ephesians says that we arm ourselves for spiritual battle. I had armed myself for this battle for so long that it was hard to put down my sword. My left hand was holding the shield of faith; my right was holding my sword. Always in church, my right hand was clenching the hilt of that sword. During August, I let go. I began to praise and worship with my hands open, arms extended, palms up toward him. Take it all, God. It's Your fight. The instant I realized that I had unclenched my hands, I heard a voice in my head, in my gut, in my spirit: "Lay down your sword, the battle is over. You will fight no more. It is broken." I sobbed. Why was He so good to me? I was so undeserving.

****

On September 17th, the six weeks were up. We were going back to Dr. Jeffries, back to the cancer center, back for another blood draw. Ding, ding. Another round. I felt myself rising up out of the ashes of defeat, but not by my power, not by my might. I was being lifted. He was the lifter of not only my head, but of our lives. He was lifting us up out of the ashes of death. I knew that no matter what happened next, it would totally be by God's hand. Either way, death or life, giving or taking away, it would only be by God's hand. We surrendered to Him; we lived the rest of the fight through him. There was such a sweet feeling in the total surrender.

We told Dr. Jeffries how well we were doing. Bob said, "I think I'm better. I'm working again, and I even played soccer!" He was happy for us.

"Let's draw light chains and see what's going on with the cancer. We'll have the results by Tuesday. Call us, and we'll let you know." He examined Bob, had blood drawn, and sent us on our way. The following Tuesday, Bob and I decided not to call for the blood test results. They didn't matter; they wouldn't change us. It was a very strange feeling, knowing that someone knew the results. Someone knew, and we didn't. We found comfort in knowing that God knew. If He wanted us to know, we would. On Friday, September 24th at 5:00 P.M., God decided it was time for us to know.

Dr. Jeffries nurse Mary called me. "Kim, this is Mary at Dr. Jeffries' office."

"Hello, Mary," I said, with a pounding heart.

"I have great news! Kim, Bob's light chains are thirty-five! That's almost normal. That's half of what they were six weeks ago! I don't know what you're doing, but keep doing it!" She sounded so happy.

"We're praying! Praise God! Thank you! Thank you! Thank you!" I hung up and cried with joy. God had done it. No drugs, no treatments. God had done it.

We were off for six more weeks. We held on to this good news for a few hours and didn't tell anyone else. It was like a present that God had given us, and we wanted to hold on to it and not share it yet! I held onto it until it wouldn't be held on to any longer. We called everyone. "God healed him!"

The kidney doctor called us the next week at home. "Kim, are you sitting down?" I was. "Bob's urine and blood tests are back. His kidney tests are all normal. His kidneys are functioning at 100%."

"What did Bob tell you?" I laughed out loud. God was so, so, so, good. "He said that God would do it."

"I remember, I remember. Good for you. Congratulations!" He was happy, too.

Another six weeks off. At the end of October Bob had blood drawn again. Again we didn't call for results. Again the doctor called us at home. Again, thirty-five.

In January of 2005, his light chains were twenty-one point nine. Our visits and blood draws were spaced to every four months. Every blood draw was normal. He was healed. Our cell group at church watched Bob slowly get better. They rejoiced with us every time we shared the good news.

One Sunday in church, our pastor asked Bob, "How are you?"

Bob told him, "I'm healed. My blood tests are getting better and better without treatment."

Bob works full-time now, and our business is thriving. Our books are not only back in the black, but we have experienced unusual growth in all areas of our business; last year we bought a new building and yard space to accommodate this newly-acquired growth. We are truly blessed. God continues to be merciful in every area that we surrendered to Him.

Twice a week Bob plays soccer with the same team that so readily accepted him back while he was still in his weakened, post-trauma state. He is actually valued as a team member again for his abilities. I had had the pleasure of watching him play and be able to tell him that he played a good game without adding the "for a guy who was half-dead a few months ago" afterward. It is utterly amazing. But, so is God.

Epilogue

It is 2009 now, almost six years since the near-death experience, and five years since God took the cancer out of Bob's body. Life is a gift.

Do we still fight? Yes, but not as often, and not always on that same battlefield.

In June of 2007, my mom, one of the strong warriors who fought by my side every day of this ordeal, was diagnosed with leukemia.

Our family, some still wounded from Bob's fight, picked up our swords and shields and battled again. God once again answered our prayers. My mother had one round of chemotherapy and told us, "I'm finished. God has healed me, and I will not have more chemotherapy." Today she is, as Bob is, cancer-free. She put her faith in God that she was healed. She is healed.

November of 2007 my daughter had a complication with her first pregnancy, our first grandson was very sick. There was a cyst in his lung that had grown large enough to cut off the growth of his heart. They endured a three month hospital stay, in-utero procedures and a lung surgery that qualified them for a T.V. news special report. Today my grandson is healthy and whole, with a fully regenerated lung!

In 2008 my dear and treasured friend Hope was diagnosed with a recurrence of cancer in her brain. She told me that she would not fight this time but was ready to go home to be with Jesus; she told me that she wanted to dance in heaven. She wrote her own obituary and peacefully, gracefully left this earth.

I don't know why we've been called to fight on this battlefield again and again. I do know that God is faithful and merciful. God has given us many gifts, but the gift of healing is one which we learned we had to fight to get. We learned to fight on the battlefield of cancer, of death. Many of us met God in a new way on this battlefield. Many of us found our healer, our provider, our strength, our comforter on this battlefield. At times we are asked to walk back onto that battleground to help others off. We go humbly. We go because we know we are called to help. We praise God who gives us strength to point others in the right direction. We walk off of the battlefield, taking the spoils, the gifts of health, with us. Whether we feel that *we* have won or lost, God is always victorious.